Switzerland
Through the Eyes of Others

Switzerland
Through the Eyes of Others

Thanh-Huyen Ballmer-Cao
Pietro Bellasi
Michael J. Enright
Shuhei Hosokawa
Claude Imbert
Natalja Ivanova
Sohan P. Modak
Michael Rutschky
Darcy Ribeiro
Ali Salem
Carol Thatcher
Daniel Vernet

Coordinating Committee for
the Presence of Switzerland Abroad

Der Alltag/Scalo

Publishers Information

Published by the Coordinating Committee for the Presence of Switzerland Abroad, 'Documentation' Group

Editorial board:
Marielle Larré, Pro Helvetia
Heinz Schwab, Swiss National Tourist Office
Hanna Widrig, Federal Department of Foreign Affairs

Project supervisor: Walter Keller
Idea and implementation: Jean Odermatt, Walter Keller
Editors: Cornelia Strasser, Gaby Weiss, Antoine Maurice

Picture editor: Giorgio J. Wolfensberger

Design: Robert & Durrer, Zurich

Production manager: Bernd Zocher, Rio Verlag Zurich

The editors would like to thank the members of the various institutions and organisations consulted for the time they spent with the authors and the hospitality they extended to them.

This publication is printed in German, French, Italian, English and Spanish.

Editorial assistants:
German: Walter Keller
English: Catherine Schelbert, Eileen Walliser-Schwarzbart, Christine Bernard, Sholto Ramsay
French: Gisèle Peter, Nicole Dervaux
Italian: Katharina Dobai
Spanish: Raquel Ruiz, Javier Mangada

Translation coordinator: Béatrice Bruchez

Translators:
German: Lorenzo Amberg, Dante Andrea Franzetti, André Kunz, Rita Peterli, Henri Schaeren, Wolfgang Eitel
English: Pamela Fritz Poynton, Gabriele Graf & Herbert R. Nestler, Margret Joss, Michael Robinson, Shaun Whiteside
French: Etienne Barilier, Elisabeth Brungger, Yvette Delaquis-Jacobsthal, Maria Graceffa, Gilbert Musy
Italian: Dino Carpinetti, Paolo Vanni, Carl Andreas Stumpf
Spanish: Maria del Mar Barea, Irene Carrillo de Albornoz, Jesús García Vera, Javier Mangada, Raquel Ruiz, Jaume Sans

Proof readers: Ursula Schweizer, Nicole Dervaux, Patrizia Oliva

Lithography: Litho AG, Aarau
Copy: Rio Verlag, Zurich
Printing: Zürichsee Medien AG, Stäfa
Binding: Buchbinderei Burkhardt AG, Mönchaltorf

Der Alltag/Scalo Verlag AG, Quellenstrasse 27, CH-8005 Zurich

©1992 Coordinating Committee for the Presence of Switzerland Abroad and Der Alltag/Scalo Verlag AG

ISBN 3-905080-20-6
ISBN 3-905080-21-4 (slipcase)

About this Book

Between December 1990 and October 1991, twelve authors from five continents were invited to explore various aspects of Switzerland. In cooperation with the publishers, they had the opportunity to study Swiss culture, economics and society. Numerous conversations with local people, visits to representative institutions and facilities, and trips to all parts of the country resulted in the present series of widely varying texts ranging from the literary travel account to the scholarly analysis and reflective essay.

- Brazilian cultural anthropologist Darcy Ribeiro deals with the way people live together in a multicultural society.
- Russian journalist Natalja Ivanova explores the complex political system of Switzerland.
- Vietnamese-born sociologist Thanh-Huyen Ballmer-Cao studies the role of women in present-day Switzerland.
- Egyptian playwright Ali Salem discovers basic facets of Swiss behaviour in the 'apple' motif of the William Tell saga.
- American Michael J. Enright, of Harvard Business School, analyses the presence of the Swiss economic sector on the national and international scene.
- Japanese cultural critic Shuhei Hosokawa takes an unusual, discreet approach to the phenomenon of Swiss banks.
- Indian molecular biologist Sohan P. Modak investigates the way a small country tackles the urgent issues of energy and ecology.
- British travel journalist Carol Thatcher views the classic holiday country of Switzerland against the backdrop of international tourism and discusses future perspectives.
- Italian sociologist Pietro Bellasi studies manifestations of day-to-day Swiss life and the mentality of the population.
- German writer Michael Rutschky casts a glance behind the Swiss façade and discovers a rich and a poor country.
- A conversation between the two French journalists Claude Imbert (Le Point) and Daniel Vernet (Le Monde) with Genevan journalist Antoine Maurice offers perspectives for Switzerland's role in a changing Europe.

The volume Through the Eyes of Others is an inquiry from outside into Switzerland, a small country rich in contrasts. The contributions not only document specific phenomena, they also point out essential aspects of the country, often from unusual angles. The texts reflect not only approval, sometimes even admiration, but also critical distance. The articles are accompanied by selected series of pictures by Swiss photographers.

Coordinating Committee for the Presence of Switzerland Abroad

Notes on the Contributors

Thanh-Huyen Ballmer-Cao
Born in Gia-Lam in Vietnam in 1951. Married to a Swiss, mother of three children. Studied political science at the University of Geneva. Habilitation (qualification to teach at university level) at the University of Zurich in 1985. 1985-1991, participation in various projects concerning the political sociology of women in Switzerland. Work on projects in the field of communal politics at the Institute of Sociology of the University of Zurich.

Pietro Bellasi
Born in Pistoia, Italy, in 1932. Studied sociology at the University of Geneva and is now a professor of sociology at the University of Bologna. Writes for various newspapers and magazines, including La Nazione, Il Tempo and Tema Celeste; broadcasts for the Italian-Swiss Radio; various exhibitions, among them 'Ipotesi Helvetia – Un certo Espressionismo'.

Michael J. Enright
Born 1958; studied economics and chemistry at Harvard, Boston/USA; doctorate in economics. Several years working on a project headed by Michael E. Porter (The Competitive Advantage of Nations). Assistant professor at Harvard Business School since 1990. Author of 'Geographic Concentration and Industrial Organization' (1990) und 'Internationale Wettbewerbsvorteile: Ein strategisches Konzept für die Schweiz' (International Competitive Advantages: A Strategic Concept for Switzerland – in collaboration with Silvio Borner, Michael E. Porter and Rolf Weder, 1991).

Shuhei Hosokawa
Born in Osaka in 1955; studied art and music in Tokyo, Zagreb and Bologna. Research assistant in musicology at the University of Tokyo, 1988-91; doctorate in 1989. Contributes essays on music, cinema, books, travel and football to international publications and anthologies; among them, 'Semiotics of Music' (1981), 'Fool for Soccer' (1989), 'Nostalgy Boulevard' (1989), 'Aesthetics of Recorded Sound' (1990), 'The Walkman-Effect' (1987).

Claude Imbert
Born in Quins, France, in 1929. Degree in philosophy/history/ethnography. Journalist since 1950, e.g. with Agence France Press, as editor-in-chief of L'Express and editor-in-chief of Paris Match. Founded the magazine Le Point with friends in 1971 and remains its editor-in-chief.

Natalja Ivanova
Born into a family of journalists in Moscow in 1945; an authority on the Russian literary scene in recent decades. Studied philology at the University of Moscow. Member of the 'April' independent association of writers. Departmental editor for the literary journal Druzhba Narodov (Friendship of Nations).

Sohan P. Modak
Born in Nasjk, India, in 1939. Doctorate in biology at the University of Geneva in 1966. Specialist in molecular biology and biotechnology. Professor of biology at the University of Poona, India, since 1979. Guest professorship at the University of Geneva, 1990-1991. Over 70 scientific publishings in international journals.

Michael Rutschky
Born in Berlin in 1943. Studied sociology, literature, philosophy and art history in Frankfurt and Berlin. Research assistant at the Free University of Berlin, 1969-77. Editor for various cultural journals. Has published several books, among them, 'Erfahrungshunger. Ein Essay über die siebziger Jahre' (Hunger for Experience. An Essay about the Seventies – 1980), 'Reise durch das Ungeschick' (Travels through Misadventure – 1990), plus photographic works and television films.

Darcy Ribeiro
Born in Montes Claros, in the Brazilian state of Minas Gerais, in 1922. Anthropologist and sociologist. Professor of Brazilian ethnography and the Tupi language in Rio de Janeiro; first vice-chancellor of the University of Brasília; politician on the national and regional level (culture and education); novelist: 'Maíra' (1980), 'Utopia Salvagem' (1986), 'O Mulo' (1990).

Ali Salem
Born in 1936; Egyptian playwright; father of three daughters. After linguistic studies and various stays abroad, 1989-90 Rockefeller Foundation fellowship in the USA at University of Michigan's Center for Near Eastern and North African Studies. His comedies, with their undertone of social criticism, are well known in the Arab world; they include 'The Wheat Well' (1968), 'Oedipus: A Comedy or You, Who Killed the Beast' (1970).

Carol Thatcher
Studied law in London. Has worked as a journalist in England and Australia since the early '80s. Travel writer, radio and television broadcaster. Her two books 'Diary of an Election' (1983, about her mother's election campaign) and 'Lloyd on Lloyd' (1985, about the marriage of tennis players Chris Evert and John Lloyd) were on the best seller lists.

Daniel Vernet
Born in Chamalières, France, in 1945. Married; lives and works in Paris. Degree from the Institut d'études politiques, Paris. Has worked as a journalist since the end of the '60s. Correspondent in Bonn, Moscow and London. Editor-in chief of the newspaper Le Monde, 1985-1991; today, head of the international relations department of the same paper. Author of the book 'Vivre à Moscou, des deux côtés du miroir' (Living in Moscow, Two Sides of the Mirror – 1978).

Notes on the Photographers

Monique Jacot (pp. 40 – 45)
Born in 1934, lives in Epesses in the wine-growing region of Vaud, where she began to photograph countrywomen in 1984. Her pictures 'Les Femmes de la terre' (Women in the country) were published in the Collection mémoire de l'oeil in 1989.

Frederic Meyer (pp. 58 – 63)
Born in 1959; after graduating from the Zurich School of Design, photographed families with their grown children in the city of Zurich in 1987.

Guido Baselgia (pp. 96 – 101)
Born in 1953, lives in Baar (Canton of Zug). Photographed the manufacture of a 164-ton turbine for a thermal power station in Taiwan in 1991. The turbine was transported from Birrfeld (Canton of Aargau) to the port of Basle by way of what is known as 'Heavy Vehicle Route No.1', which leads along small roads and through villages in northwestern Switzerland.

Max Schmid (pp. 134 – 139)
Born in 1945, lives in Winterthur. The earth's surviving original landscapes constitute his chief photographic interest. In 1991 he photographed one of the last primeval forests of Europe, the region between the Muotatal (Canton of Schwyz) and the Klöntal (Canton of Glarus).

Nicolas Faure (pp. 154 – 159)
Born in 1949, lives in Geneva. Two years working and hiking to capture on film the erratic boulders in built-up areas left behind when the glaciers retreated.

Peter Maurer (pp. 179 – 185)
Born in 1963, lives in Dachsen (Canton of Zurich). Has paid regular visits to the rural, pre-alpine culture of Appenzell with his large-format camera since 1985.

Michael and Richard Aschwanden
(pp. 198 – 201)
The Uri photographer Michael Aschwanden (1865 – 1940) began documenting the pre-industrial era in the Canton of Uri in 1898. The photographs his son Richard (born in 1909) took of the same views in 1985 show the changes tourism and traffic have wrought in the region.

Other photographers

Emanuel Ammon, Lucerne 67; Giorgio von Arb, Zurich 52; Derek Bennett, Schaffhausen 16; Ursula Markus, Zurich 21; Koni Nordmann, Zurich 109, 118; Jean Odermatt, Eglisau, cover; Heini Stucki, Tschugg 30, 37, 49, 69, 72, 74, 128/129; Werner Hauser, Winterthur 175; Andreas Wolfensberger, Winterthur 149, 165, 193.

Table of Contents

Switzerland and 'Swissness'
Darcy Ribeiro

In 1884, the explorer Karl von Steinen became the first European to penetrate the Central Brazilian jungles around the headwaters of the Rio Xingu. In his account, *Through Central Brazil*, he reported his amazement at happening upon a wild 'federation of peoples' – 'wild' by definition, because the federation was made up of 'native peoples', and yet highly cultivated.

On this occasion and during a subsequent expedition, the ethnologist encountered ten Indian peoples whose languages derived from quite different stocks and who were utterly incomprehensible to one another. Each of the peoples maintained its own tribal identity and took pride in it, and yet they lived peacefully together.

Over centuries of coexistence the cultures of these Indian peoples had come to show an extraordinary resemblance. They all lived in large huts arranged in a circle around a wide central courtyard in which dances and sporting competitions took place. They all had tame eagles, imprisoned in huge cages made of longsticks. Their women wore a tiny, five-square-centimetre *Uluri* which covered only their private parts but was still held to be an item of clothing because they would have felt quite naked without it, and more importantly because any man who touched it ran the risk of sustaining a withered hand. The tribes lived chiefly on manioc, which was planted in the surrounding forests, and on fish caught in the rivers where they lived. They also ate monkeys and a few species of bird, but otherwise they avoided meat almost entirely.

Each group in the Xingu region had specialised in the manufacture of a product which it exchanged with the others. They all used the same pottery, the same bows and arrows, and even their hammocks and necklaces were identical. Periodically they organised large gatherings at which members of the various tribes met in a village for the solemn commemoration of a deceased loved one, but principally to exchange manufactured products and take part in sporting events, such as wrestling or spear-throwing. Trade and sporting activity had replaced war.

When I visited these Indians seventy years later, I discovered that their almost unbelievable, peaceful coexistence had been preserved intact. Despite the onslaughts of civilisation the Indian peoples had maintained their fine, partnership-based culture.

I am reminded of this admirable cooperation whenever I think of Switzerland. Switzerland, too, is a conglomerate of people who, without any theory of statehood, have learned to cooperate and yet to maintain their own identity. Both modi vivendi – on the tribal level and on an extremely advanced level – belong to an emerging society of the future, which is clearly not our own, for we have so far succeeded only in setting people against each other. But, although it is as yet invisible to us, it has already shown us some of its salient features. One of these, I believe, is the ability to establish large macro-national formations, which will unite the fates of many previously hostile nations, like the heralded European or the North American federations.

Another feature is the room that is opening up to micro-ethnic groups and oppressed nationalities to find their own identity and fight for their political autonomy. Never before have these peoples been granted so many freedoms, but neither have they ever before insisted so radically on their autonomy and independence.

For this new society, the experience of the peaceful, tribal coexistence of the Indian peoples of the Xingu is of crucial importance, but even more important is the Swiss experience of the coexistence of 4 groups of people who speak different languages and live, in 3 variants of Western culture, in a tiny area, surrounded by powerful neighbours who are finally preparing to coexist in peace.

Everywhere in the world there are conglomerates of diverse people obliged to live together under repressive conditions; unified states in which territorial power over everyone is exercised by the imposed leadership of a particular region. In states such as these, the rebellion of countless peoples raises a crucial question – the question of the restructuring of unified states.

They contrast starkly with the peaceful tribal life of the Indians of the Xingu, or the harmonious coexistence of the people in the Swiss Confederation. But in a world where conflict is the norm, Switzerland has so far been the great exception.

The Lesson of Switzerland

What can we learn from these exemplary instances of peaceful coexistence? Most importantly, they do not demand assimilation. No Xingu Indian, no Swiss citizen has any desire to force anybody to adopt his way of thinking or to give up his ethnic identity. Mutual respect and tolerance allow others the freedom to be themselves, however different they may be. The direction taken by the Xingu Indians runs counter to the conventional course of development. Societies normally develop through warlike conflicts; the equality and solidarity of the tribal federation are brought to an end so that everyone can be put to work.

Through slavery or paid labour, the mass of people produce more than they consume so that a minority can live the good life. The Indians of the Xingu have refused to take this course. For them the simple, good and peaceful life has become the meaning of life itself. They have created a small, naked, happy and stable society. Without civilisation's invasions they could go on living like this for thousands of years without having to do any work in the sense of commodity production; they would be concerned solely with the joy of living, with promoting cooperation and with further adaptation to the forest and rivers where they live. The Swiss have not achieved the perfection of this tropical paradise and they never will in their freezing-cold country. But they still have the motivation to get up early every day and go about their difficult working routines, supporting, serving and even loving their husbands or wives and producing more Swiss citizens. They have a talent for achieving happiness just so long as it doesn't disturb the lives of others too much.

This way of life dates back to a pact drawn up 700 years ago, when some of the ancestors of today's Swiss agreed to resolve their problems exclusively among themselves. Since then nobody has interfered in the affairs of the Swiss. They alone decide – sometimes rightly, sometimes wrongly – by means of discussions and votes. Votes are taken on the most trivial matters. Switzerland is the country of consensus.

Switzerland was formed from the unification of three cantons of farmers and craftsmen, united against the nobility and the clergy. The rebels also defended the right of passage and freedom of trade on the alpine highways, because that was, even then, their chief livelihood. This pact contained the seeds from which the Swiss institutions of today were to grow. It is based on five fundamental principles:

• the refusal to accept or enforce any pre-eminence in internal affairs,
• unlimited solidarity in defence against external enemies,
• the right to freedom of passage and freedom of trade on the basis of trustworthiness,
• national votes as an instrument of political life,
• neutrality in foreign conflicts, but without a fanaticism that would obstruct international cooperation.

The alliance, free of ethnic, linguistic and religious constraints, in fact served as a basis for the later voluntary amalgamation with other communes, until the country evolved into its present form. The organisation of Switzerland was based on civil ties that turned the inhabitants of a particular territory into citizens. The pride of the nation, then, is this historic pact, from which Switzerland emerged through a civil act of will.

The Xingu alliance and the Swiss Confederation are both based on civil and ethnic bonds – the strongest means of soldering human communities together. Both are only possible in the long run because their unity is based on respect for their multi-ethnic city, and the ethnocentricities in each are preserved but at the same time kept within bounds.

Their unity is also based on the fact that local, community and national territory form the basis for the definition of state citizenship. When we examined the survival of hundreds of native Brazilian tribes – some consisting of not more than a dozen people – we observed that a race is destroyed only if families break down, thus interrupting the continuity of identification created by educating children in the tradition of the parents.

Neither a mixture of races, however pronounced it may be, nor enforced acculturation, which is inevitable if these tribes are surrounded by a civilising context, can liquidate a native tribe. In the face of every affliction, the tribes have remained true to themselves over the centuries and maintained their identification as a single people, different from all others and in opposition to all others.

Little attention has been paid to the effectiveness of this ethnic bond because of the predominance of Marxist interpretations, which held class struggle to be the sole motor of history. But Marxist interpretations were wrong. Inter-ethnic tensions are not only older than class struggles, but in many cases even more important. That they are older is revealed by the fact that societies first consisted of peoples or tribes of various racial groups, and they lived in peace only very seldom, long before it was possible for them to be divided into classes. The ethnic components are also more important because the call of the fatherland was often stronger than class solidarity, as we can see from various European wars. The proletariat never managed to unite across national boundaries to fight against the bourgeoisie.

Contrasts and Comparisons

It was not until 1848, after a religious war, that fortunately never escalated, that modern Switzerland emerged as a plebiscitary state. It was based on the communally exercised sovereignty of a multi-national organisation which turned into a nation. The constitution drawn up at that time was the instrument that made the Swiss cantons finally abandon any claims to hegemony. The Swiss established a common area of political institutions, which they used henceforward to determine their fate. For one hundred years or so they have been celebrating the historic date 1291 as a baptismal certificate, and also as the fiction of a 700-year tradition, their 'Mayflower'. And quite rightly so, for no other nation has achieved anything remotely comparable. But since the Xingu Indians have also taken the same path, it must, admittedly, be an accessible one, albeit quite rare and unusual. The many attempts to assert its practicability have been failures, one and all. These were all multi-ethnic states with a supra-national mission, but they lacked the bonding agent required to keep them together as federal nations.

Swissness

The Spanish talk a lot about hispanidad, the proud and almost arrogant feeling of being a Spaniard. Can we speak in a similar sense, if more subtly, of 'Swissness'?
The Swiss say no. They are forever claiming that there is no such thing as the Swiss as such, precisely because Switzerland as such does not exist. In a concrete sense, the Swiss exist as a diverse combination of people who each speak a dialect of a particular mother tongue, who pray in the church of a particular religion and live in a particular commune of a particular canton, or come from one. Everything is quite precise, but defined in a local framework.
Yet I think things are otherwise. Behind this modesty there lies the deep pride in being Swiss – every Helvetic citizen's cherished heritage. One thing is certain – I've put this one to the test – the Swiss have a tendency to speak, tirelessly and always with a hint of false modesty, of the exotic aspects of their highly civilised nation. They talk at length about the democratic nature of their people, the actual power of the autonomous local governments, the beauty and quality of the cows, the cheese and almost everything else.
Certainly, there are minor differences between the German Swiss and the French Swiss, the inhabitants of Ticino and the Rhaeto-Romans, but no major ones. If we compare them not with each other but with some other, non-Swiss people, their essential unity is unmistakable. This observation is borne out by the fact that throughout the whole of Switzerland there is one highly developed cult to which everybody is most passionately devoted. It is

nothing more or less than patriotism. This typically Swiss patriotism appears at the regional and even the communal level, so that every Swiss is a citizen of his canton, and within it, a citizen of his commune, his little fatherland.

The efforts of the Swiss to respect these local contexts are extraordinary; they are becoming the voice of the nation. Consequently the canton within the country and the commune within the canton are granted the greatest respect and autonomy.

I came across an impressive illustration of this tendency during a nationwide debate over the legality of crucifixes in the classrooms of state schools, which a commune in Ticino wanted to have judicially enforced. Public debates raged, as the case moved from one judicial authority to the next. Finally the highest court delivered its verdict. It granted the commune in question – but only that commune – the right to hang crucifixes in its school buildings! The Swiss do not see the canton as an administrative district, but rather as a governmental region, which, along with others, forms the nation. It is held to be of great importance. We might describe the Swiss canton as a miniature nation guarding its own autonomy, which the Swiss have so wonderfully enforced.

Even centralistically-minded Napoleon refused to divide up the Swiss cantons and annex them to adjoining countries. He described this exceptional situation as follows: 'The more I have studied the geography, history, and customs of your country, the more I am convinced that it should never be made subject to a central government and uniform laws. Such a diverse country needs diversity of government. The federal system, which is contrary to the interest of large states because it fragments their strength, is very favourable to smaller ones, because it leaves them with all their natural vigour. Zurich will be defended by the people of Zurich, Berne will have its Bernese and the little cantons will have the children of William Tell.'

There are certainly fears that the German Swiss could become too dominant in terms of internal politics because they are the strongest national group and enjoy great economic success internationally. But the peculiarity of Switzerland lies in the unusual fact that German-, Italian-, French- and Rhaeto-Roman-speaking people, people of Catholic, Protestant or Jewish faith, live in peace; no integrative pressure is exerted on others, nor is there any need to renounce one's own individuality.

In fact, the Swiss are being confronted with a new situation that leaves them feeling somewhat apprehensive. In the past, the other Europeans would be ruined by war every twenty years and had to start all over again, while Switzerland, thanks to its neutrality, remained intact. There hasn't been a war in Europe for 40 years now. Consequently the Germans, French and Italians are enjoying glowing prosperity. Switzerland has also visibly prospered in the post-war period. But in their emotional reaction the Swiss remind me of those old Brazilian families who held onto their estates and even increased their herds of cattle and yet felt frustrated because much richer bankers and industrialists had popped up next to them.

There are other reasons why the Swiss might be feeling a degree of insecurity, which has over the past few years led them to talk in terms of a crisis. When I look at the figures for

the constantly increasing wealth of Switzerland and compare them with those of other countries, even the very wealthiest, I can't see a crisis. I am even inclined to deny that there is one. But so insistent were they that I have to admit, in the end, that this is the dominant mood in the country.

If we struggle for an explanation, what can we come up with? What disappointments and frustrations can be seen in Switzerland's most recent history? As you always find something if you look hard enough, I finally found a few reasons.

One important frustration that struck me was the disappointment of the Swiss where politics are concerned. A few years ago the ball was set rolling with a scandal in which the Minister of Justice covered up for her husband, a lawyer, when he was accused of laundering drug money. Here was the Switzerland of Red Cross renown, dragged through the mud by being associated with the drug trade, and all this was aggravated by the damage being done to another jewel in the Helvetian crown, the rectitude of the Swiss bankers.

The biggest thorn in Switzerland's flesh has probably been a furious politician who tirelessly writes apocalyptic articles and books which the Swiss secretly take to heart, because he shows how and why Switzerland 'washes whiter'. I refer to the Swiss Member of Parliament Jean Ziegler, who wrote in El Pais on 17 December 1990: 'Switzerland will for many years to come be a centre for the laundering of murderous money. Everything predisposes it to this: the lack of any law forbidding this lucrative business, a hermetic secrecy in banking, superior competence and the multinational organisation of its most important business banks, the cynicism and amorality of a large number of its bankers, working in a small country which has no raw materials, and which is in the difficult situation of having to compete with the big banking empires of the biggest European states. All the techniques of receipt, disguise and transfer of money from organised crime into financial circulation are currently being used in Switzerland – and in other parts of the world.'

As if such charges were not enough, another national scandal broke out when the newspapers accused the government of keeping files on a large number of Swiss citizens, both good and bad. The idea that respectable, honourable people and crooks were being lumped together filled the country with horror. Further terrors were provoked by the news that certain groups were actually organising a secret army without the knowledge of the government. Venial sins, I would say as a Brazilian, accustomed to political despotism, corruption, nepotism and exemptions from punishment. Not so the Swiss, who cannot cope with these scandals in their own family.

Causes for Concern

The basic problem behind this sense of crisis reveals another Swiss speciality: perfectionism. That, at any rate, is the opinion of one Swiss intellectual who has been studying the national character of his compatriots. According to him, the Swiss live in constant dissatisfaction with themselves, so as to hone their critical awareness and push themselves towards new limits. These unflagging self-doubts and self-accusations, as well as a certain pleasure in revealing supposed errors and minutely investigating the causes of an occasional failure, are the chief characteristics of the Swiss. My Swiss source thinks that this critical awareness, this urge for self-perfection, is what protects the country from the ever-present threat of withering away complacently in a world that is constantly evolving.

That may be so, but I find that kind of strenuous virtue wearisome and anyway, I have my doubts about it. I need to see real shortcomings. And I think I've found one, too: the indifference of the Swiss towards the fate of other countries. I wanted to find out whether Switzerland not only has an interest in perfecting its already high standard of living, but also a concrete interest in opening up new horizons of life and happiness for the human race as a whole. I found nothing. Switzerland, already perfect, is wearing itself out refining that perfection.

I first had the impression of a 'finished' country when I visited Switzerland in 1954. I spent two months in Geneva, which was in those days less rich but in my eyes overwhelmingly beautiful.

My first jolt came when I saw a bunch of fresh tulips every evening in the window of the butcher's shop that I passed on the way back to my hotel. It almost left me speechless. The second jolt, which cured me of my stupidity, came when a friend took me with him to the Jura. I, the savage, saw a whole forest there filled with nothing but almost identical trees. But my astonishment turned into annoyance when I noticed the aluminium plaques with numbers, showing when the trees were to be felled and sawn up. Terrible. For me, that was the ultimate, incontestable proof that I was in a complete, finalised almost perfect country, and I found that quite appalling. I then felt a foolish pride in coming from a country that still waited to be built. Coming from Amazonia, with its greatly varied jungles, which I had travelled through months before, around the headwaters of the Maracaçume River, I saw Switzerland as a country in its final stages. Today I would prefer to speak of a finished country. It is so perfectly complete that they might as well pension off everybody in Switzerland, because there's no need for them any more.

During my stay on that occasion I was also able to experience how Swiss institutions work, guaranteeing each citizen his or her inalienable, constitutional rights. One day, having lunch with a diplomat, I suddenly found myself surrounded by policemen who had been called to the house and who had arrested and interrogated the housekeeper. The lovely Swiss francs that my friend was missing hadn't been stolen by his wife or his very young children, the policemen said. No! It was the Italian housekeeper, who had been caught in flagrante. There was no doubt that she was the thief. But just how much of a thief was she? She admitted to having stolen 920 francs. But my friend had spoken to the police about more than 2,000. He tried to rectify his estimate, so as not to be caught thieving from the thief. But the police didn't accept his less than plausible explanations. Swiss men know exactly how much money they have in their wallets. Without the shadow of a doubt! Lucky things!

Because of this intuitively perceived contrast between Swiss reality and our own, every time I come to Geneva I visit the Calvin Memorial in the university. It's wonderful! But I think I only look at it so often to call to mind the Protestant preacher's Brazilian utopia. In fact, it was Calvin who provided the impulse for the original founding of Rio de Janeiro. He supported an expedition of over 800 Huguenots and other believers who had gone there in 1555 in order to found a pure and pious community in the Bay of Guanabara. When they arrived, the holy men immediately found themselves surrounded by beautiful, shamelessly naked Indian women. The women declared their willingness to get involved with the travellers just as soon as they had rid themselves of that smell they had, typical of white people and made much worse by the long sea journey. Many of the men immediately jettisoned their pious intentions and succumbed to the sins of the flesh; some of them were even hanged.

But this Genevan utopia was finished off by the Jesuits, who wanted to convert my poor Indians likewise, but on behalf of the Pope. The Jesuits signed up as many friendly Indians as they could, and set them on the Indians befriended by the Calvinists. In this war between Reformation and Counter-Reformation over 10,000 Indians lost their lives without knowing why, along with some twenty whites who had not fled in time. What would this Calvinist utopia have turned into? A tropical Switzerland?

Only on Sunday should one not visit the Calvin Memorial. There are a lot of churches in the area, and a lot of God-fearing Swiss coming out of them. Throughout the week they have a quite different facial expression, they look practical, serious and hearty. Industrious as they are, they spend their time manufacturing enormous turbines and tiny watches. They produce advanced computers and automatic dolls that can speak, sing and dance. All this perfect, well-ordered world lacks is perfect happiness. Oh, if only the Swiss could be freed from their fears.

The greatest threat to the Swiss lies in their achievement of a completely perfect society. For that reason the Swiss, it seems to me, need to invent artificial motivations and stimuli to perfection so that their creative impulses stay alive and their relative positions are maintained. In fact, what is there for the Swiss to do? Everything's already been done. Is that why so many happy Swiss commit suicide, out of pure happiness? It saddens me that the Swiss are blind to the enormous range of activity that lies before them in this sad world while generous activities would bring Switzerland dignity and a deeper sense of humanity. What frightens me most is the fact that the Swiss are so apathetic and indifferent.

But whenever I look not only at them, but at all the other rich Europeans and try to understand them, what startles me is that in heeding the call of the Greens they pay attention only to saving their own gardens, and the gardens of their neighbours. Certainly the Swiss are also worried about the extraordinary destructive power of their industry, which threatens to ruin their landscape. Is that, shall we say, the situation of contemporary Europe, a Europe that has had enough wars but also enough utopias? The fate of mankind no longer concerns them; it doesn't move anybody any more.

All Europeans, and the Swiss more than anybody else, are firmly convinced that their country is doing a considerable amount to help the poor nations of the world. They can neither understand that for each dollar spent there they reap four or five in return, nor do they notice that the economic relationship forced on the poor countries is one of the causes of the hunger and backwardness of our people.

But the bankers, who know a great deal about it, want to comfort us with the argument that our ruling classes take a mighty share of all the profits. That's right! They're the ones who are turning our peoples into an offshore proletariat of the richer world. We have always been seen as a collection of businesses, chaining our people in to produce the sugar that sweetens European mouths, finding gold that makes them rich and growing coffee that perks them up. Recently we have been producing mountains of soya as mast for their pigs and at the same time drastically reducing the production of beans, the chief source of nourishment of our people.

These are facts, and I could mention other terrible things, but it isn't appropriate since my subject today is the Swiss! I refer to their obtuseness when faced with the fact that we, the poor nations, are the capital exporters of this world. It's easy to prove if you count up how much we have exported in terms of goods and commodities throughout the whole post-war period and what we have received in return. Obviously we have given the rich nations many times what they have given us. It strikes me as almost diabolical that we get further and further into debt thanks to the cunning of their bankers, and in the process increase their wealth at the cost of our own poverty and backwardness. It's enough to make you weep. Such egoism and greed on the part of the profiteers, such cold indifference – might they not be due to the premature ageing of the Europeans, the Swiss included?

Children and Old People

The most striking thing about the Swiss human landscape where the Brazilian visitor is concerned is the high proportion of old people. You hardly ever see any children and if you do they look like adults. What might be the reason for that? If the average age is rising from just above twenty to over fifty, it means that, in a population that can't maintain its present level, there are practically no children left: the well-fed people in the street have a sad look about them.

When I took a good, clear look at the country, on the lookout less for the beauties of Switzerland than for its shortcomings, I found a few more. What immediately surprised me, apart from the lack of children, was a certain dislike of children. It may not be so, but when I considered the Swiss in those terms I had the impression that they much prefer their cats and dogs to their children. I also had the feeling they don't much like young people. Is that so? Young people are obviously seen as being chiefly a potential threat, to older Swiss citizens and to the fatherland. Like the children, the young people aren't showered with extravagant affection. They are little creatures awaiting domestication, passing through Piaget's developmental phases on their way to blossoming into good Swiss citizens. The dogs and cats are the really lucky ones, coddled and cosseted by everybody.

The eventful youth riots in 1980 were all hushed-up, peacefully and not so peacefully. In a serious society like Switzerland there's no room for youthful rebellion. Young people are supposed to study and prepare themselves for the burden of full civil responsibility, later,

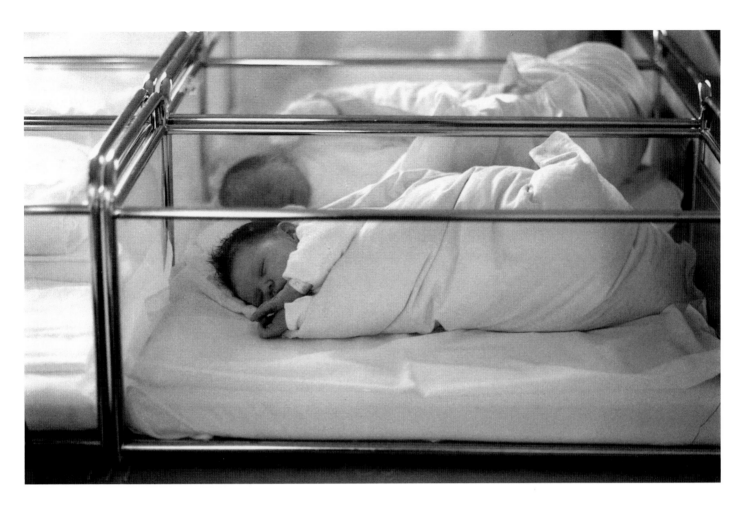

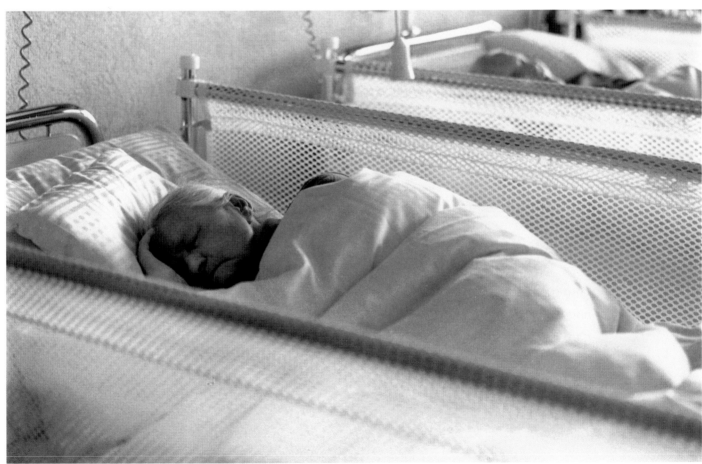

when it's their turn! But until then they should keep quiet and enjoy themselves within the established limits of good order.

Switzerland has a considerable number of drug addicts, perishing in the anti-orgasm of cocaine and heroin. I saw them in a square in Zurich, packed together, abandoned and left to their fate. Despite the cold weather at the time there were about two hundred of them. When it gets warmer their numbers probably swell ten times. Are there other squares like that? These people probably get help the minute they declare themselves ready to return to the bourgeois lifestyle.

Since they're neither able nor willing to do so, there's little to be done. Certainly it could be even worse, because there's always somebody who wants drug addicts to be arrested on the spot. Leaving them to their own devices in the middle of Zurich is showing too much tolerance as far as a lot of Swiss are concerned.

The high proportion of old people in Switzerland is something new. A few generations ago the average age was fairly low. The women often brought a lot of children into the world. So many, that for centuries Switzerland had an exportable population surplus for which there was not enough work in the country. Since the last war, however, Switzerland has been importing workers. Today there are over 1,120,000 of them, an enormous number for a population of just seven million inhabitants.

Most of them are single men, and that in itself explains the sadness with which they watch the many beautiful and inaccessible Swiss girls. The foreign workers are treated as if they were only living here temporarily, with a view to going back home as quickly as possible. But that's not how it is. They are indispensable, because without them production and the high standard of living could no longer be maintained.

For a long time I've kept an eye out for poor people in Switzerland. As it was clear to me that they weren't on display to the tourists, I thought I would find them in ghettos, in poorer quarters. I never saw a single one. Does the golden rule actually work, according to which every single poor person manages to get back home to his village and receive the support he needs when his life is in ruins? I don't know. It's part of the Swiss religion. Perhaps it works for those who admit their failure and return home, sad and contrite. Small consolation for my insatiable heart.

Things to Envy

Having spoken about the possible shortcomings of Switzerland and the Swiss, we might now talk about its advantages over other nations. The most enviable thing about the country, in my opinion, is the extraordinary delight that the Swiss take in voting. The classical concept according to which the commonweal is the aim of politics and the will of the people is expressed in votes, has almost assumed an exaggerated form in Switzerland. Votes are constantly being taken about everything on a national, cantonal and communal level. The citizens are called to participate in every decision that could affect them directly. They vote, for example, on whether to renovate old or build new schools or railway stations. They vote on the right of women to vote, which was introduced very late because the majority of male voters had to declare their agreement in advance.

Recently a vote was taken on nothing less serious than the abolition of the army, which is the pride of the Swiss. Those who wanted to get rid of the regular army wanted to prove to the world that armies are utterly superfluous and much too dangerous to be constantly ready for battle. But it didn't work. Only 35 per cent were in favour. It hasn't worked yet. But who knows. We may, one fine day, have a Switzerland without weapons.

Those are the major issues that everybody ought to vote on, so that they aren't left to the politicians. But the Swiss also vote on a lot of trifling matters and sometimes they make the wrong decisions. The citizens of Zurich, the biggest and richest city in Switzerland, recently voted on whether the young people should be allowed to stay in the old city building they had occupied as a cultural and leisure centre. The people of Zurich voted against it.

Another likeable trait of the Swiss is their disregard for heroes, generals and political leaders. They are quite unshakeable in their claims that they have never had any. They even like to point out that the saga of their mythical national hero William Tell came from the pen of a German poet. One Swiss commentator, taking this idea of equality to the limit, even claimed that 'great men', beside whom normal people would look like dwarves, don't exist in Switzerland.

It isn't true, of course. Zwingli was a contemporary of Luther. Calvin, a citizen of Geneva by choice, captured the public imagination. Jean-Jacques Rousseau – that's right, the one with the 'noble savage' and the principle of choice – was Swiss. In modern educational theory there are great names such as Pestalozzi, Claparède and Piaget; in art Le Corbusier and Paul Klee and countless others. Paracelsus was Swiss, and his tradition still continues. There have been eighteen Swiss winners of the Nobel Prize. Not long ago a Swiss citizen developed the computer language Pascal, and another invented the indispensable computer 'mouse'.

We can mention a host of lesser achievements, but beware, they'll make us green with envy. I most envy the Swiss of their educational system. The communes are responsible for this: they design the curriculum, they build and run the schools. They also produce an enormous number of school books so that every child understands that he couldn't have come into the world in a better place than this very commune and that he has something to be proud of. All Swiss children between the ages of six and fifteen are assured a school place, and the attention of an admirable body of teachers. The country's high-school teaching has won international respect for its efficiency. How could we not go green with envy?

Even if I'm growing weary of delivering eulogies, I should still mention how energetically the Swiss rise to the challenges of our time. Despite having a traditionally puritanical, Calvinistic family structure, the revolution of female sexuality, encouraged by the pill and the right to orgasm, has to a large extent become a reality. A permissiveness unthinkable a generation before has taken root in Switzerland and radically redefined the concept of sin, although not to such an extent that a young Swiss girl might not suffer from guilt feelings inherited from her puritanical grandmother, or would have no regrets if her feminist commitment occasionally proved successful.

In the cities many women have exchanged the hearth for the workplace, and are leaving their children, where possible, to the mechanical care of the crèches or the tutelage of the school. Hardly anyone nowadays would condemn the single mothers who were mercilessly persecuted in the past. Parents, newly permissive, no longer object if young people take their pleasure in a room somewhere at home. Motels for secret rendez-vous have become practically redundant.

Another great achievement is the successful treatment of television. The Swiss have shown a high level of moral responsibility and educational commitment in this field. Given the particular conditions of the country, the German Swiss, who are both wealthier and more numerous, help to fund the official French- and Italian-language Swiss television stations to guarantee a measure of equality. Sometimes the indefatigable Swiss complain about the excess of violence and sex on their television screens. In their innocence they don't know what they're doing. I can imagine the scandal if they had to watch the idol of children and adults in Brazil, Xuxa, luring seven-year-old children into erotically charged skirmishes before the eyes of millions of enthusiastic viewers.

What impressed me most of all was the efficiency with which Swiss television leads its viewers into other cultural areas such as cinema, theatre, music and the visual arts. Here in Brazil every channel anaesthetises its viewers daily with three to four hours of melodramatic soap operas, leaving them with neither the time nor the desire for anything else.

Things European

There are deeper, more substantial reasons for the shock to the Swiss system which has led to the widespread awareness of a national crisis. Chief among them is the country's urgently needed, almost inevitable integration into the European Community. The Swiss even rejected membership of the United Nations, but since they have no longer an excuse for escaping European integration, they are suffering.

Their most important economic partners are the European states. If Switzerland were to close itself off, the Europeans would establish closer relations with other partners. Integration is thus inevitable, and doesn't seem much of an inconvenience, given the financial power of Switzerland and its high level of technological development – both necessary preconditions for successful integration.

The only disadvantages would be to Swiss agriculture, which is basically a subordinate interest. In order to approach the ideal of self-sufficiency, Swiss agriculture is being run in such a way that it can not survive without major subsidies. The beautiful Swiss cows, the pride of the nation because of their appearance, their excellent milk and cheese, cost the Swiss more than their opera stars. As the chief purpose of the cows is to act as staffage in the bucolic landscape and delight the tourists, Switzerland's hoteliers could fund their upkeep without infringing the rules of the European Community.

The ultimate cheek as far as the Swiss are concerned is the compulsory nature of the European Community. They don't like obeying directives from above, or bowing to circumstance. European integration is the requirement of the moment; it is a fundamental precondition for the long-term existence and prosperity of Switzerland. That is what causes the Swiss more heartache than anything else. It pains them so much that they are saddened by the progress advancing towards their previously unbreachable boundaries. And in fact the most impenetrable mountain ranges and forests have been made available for economic exploitation. Consequently the centripetal motion that has been drawing everyone into the industrial centre is now reversing: the Swiss are being forced outwards and 'foreigners' are being drawn into the country.

There are also certain fears about the inevitable German dominance of a future Europe. In the eyes of many Swiss, Germany, which failed over two world wars to put its dreams of power into practice, seems to be on the verge of achieving supremacy, not through force of arms but through economic superiority.

Utterly without any predilection for ideological internationalism, the Swiss are suspicious of the cosmopolitanism flapping about their ears. It is unsettling, particularly as it is emerging from the capitalism of the European Community, just when the collapse of proletarian internationalism has become apparent. What is likely to be the result? The Swiss have always had a lot of time for mercantile, technological and most importantly financial internationalism. But they are turning against all other forms of internationalism, apart, perhaps, from some charitable development aid.

Worse than anything else is the apprehensiveness with which they are asking themselves: What is this Europe – a nation made of nations – that is coming into being? Is it a reliable economic alliance? Or is it only a banking corporation made up of rich and poor members in which a fantastically rich Germany may have too much power?

How will the European Community look as a political power? Will it be a colonial-style imperialism, a totalitarianism in the classic Soviet mould or like a big version of Switzerland? How elastic will this supranational Europe be?

The Central European core can be precisely defined, but there is a whole marginal area that is far from unambiguous. Nobody wishes to deny the Greeks their membership of Europe; after all they founded it. But are the Turks Europeans as well? If they are, then the Algerians and Moroccans on the other side of the Mediterranean are even more so. Will the European Community only be a new mediterranes mare nostrum? Or will it extend to Europeanised Africa? Why should Latin America not be included as well, the biggest population of Romance people, more European than many Europeans? 'Who shall we mix with?' the Swiss ask themselves helplessly. Switzerland is afraid of being required to become a component part of this vaguely outlined and 'unfinished' community which could go in unforeseen directions.

At the end of this essay, which has been nothing if not ambitious, I should like to point out that there are good and bad problems in our all too imperfect world. The problems of the Swiss are without a doubt among the good problems, the enviably good ones.

Switzerland: 'European, but still with its mountains …'
Natalja Ivanova

Switzerland is an experiment that was started in 1291 by a group of resolute men with the obvious co-operation of their God. It is an experiment that, carried through with the utmost precision, had stood the test of time and is still continuing today (even though, I think, the Swiss themselves do not realise it).

Switzerland lies at the heart of Europe like the filigree egg of a an inspired jeweller, carefully packed in snow-white cotton wool and tucked securely in the jewel-box of the Alps.

The tension eases somewhat, and the customs official's answering smile to my accent only appears after he is convinced that I shall soon be leaving the hallowed land. The Swiss seem to think that everybody wishes to become Swiss.

It brings back hazy memories of a thick pre-Revolutionary Russian children's encyclopaedia in the family for generations, which contained a special article: *On the Snowpeaks of Switzerland*. There were engravings: the legendary William Tell with his son snuggled close to him; the cruel Bailiff Gessler, with the power of life and death over others, and finally, 'The Fighters for Freedom': 'When oppression reached its height, the Swiss resolved to make a stand. Three bold leaders called their trustworthy companions to a lonely meadow, the Rütli Meadow, where they formed a lasting alliance and swore to defend forever the freedom of their fatherland.'

Freedom has been Switzerland's most enduring value. In the inner courtyard of the City Hall in Basel, I read an inscription painted in bright red, gold, blue and green which livens up the pale January light. It must surely stem from the Middle Ages: 'Freedom is more than silver and gold.'

The swift and noiseless Intercity train between Zurich and Geneva passes high up above Lake Geneva. Our eyes feast on the splendid panorama of mountain peaks, tranquil lake surface and vineyards terraced down to the water. A pretty picture postcard? Yes, that is the first impression; the scenery is almost too glossy. Political incidents? Dear, oh dear! Of course. You'll be told, for instance, about the hundreds of thousands of supposedly suspect citizens who were spied upon by the police; about the first woman federal councillor who had to resign for relaying confidential information to her husband; about the 'secret army', an undercover organisation whose intention was to save Switzerland in the event of a totalitarian invasion. Those are the political incidents of the past few years.

And suddenly one feels in Switzerland, whose outline can be likened to the tiny heart of Europe, as if one were deep in the provinces, travelling with Grandmother to Grandfather for a breath of fresh air after the bad dream of the big city.

But what is the reason for this silence, this stillness? The character of the people? Can one speak of a uniform Swiss character when, as the Swiss sociologist André Siegfried quite rightly observed, the Swiss-German people tend to be orderly, sensible, diligent, scrupulously honest, imperturbable and reliable whereas the French-Swiss incline more to general principles and abstract things, are more emotional and dynamic but at the same time more practical? If, meanwhile, we study the 'popularity polls' that examine how linguistic and religious groups feel about each other, we recognise a high degree of uniformity among the Swiss. Is the reason for peace and quiet to be found in the stability of the political and social organisations they have created rather than in the national character?

The Confederation was originally a military and economic union of three regions formed as a defence against invasion. By the beginning of the 16th century, 13 cantons had joined this union for mutual support. They had no common administration or army, not even a standard currency. And one can hardly say that unity and democracy triumphed from the beginning! The cantons did not have equality. Aargau and Vaud were subjugated by wealthy Berne, Uri demanded tribute from Ticino. Vassal cantons then - not very democratic, is it? If cantons wanted to discuss an issue with each other, a meeting place was arranged since there was no capital in the old Confederation. These diets formed the basis of the future parliament. Up to the end of the 18th century there was only an advisory body. Not until after a civil war in the 1840s were the federal structures established and incorporated in the Constitution of 1848, which has in essence survived to this day.

Switzerland's famous neutrality is not due to the fact that the Swiss national character is particularly placid. We must remember that the Swiss were notorious for their boldness, their strength and their military arts; they served in the armies of many a nation, including Russia. However, without neutrality there would be no Switzerland. Just suppose for a moment that Switzerland was not neutral. Some cantons would be united with France and would follow her politics while others would be with Germany. In the event of a conflict in Europe or in Switzerland, neutrality is unanimously supported by all cantons. The Swiss are neutral because they 'neutralise' each other.

And the stillness?

No, not just the dense, palpable silence of the majestic Alps towering above alpine lakes that reflect their snowcapped peaks. I attended a session of the Federal Assembly in Berne and found the quiet most impressive, especially after the clamorous debates in our parliament.

The members took their seats, each among their own party of which there are more than a dozen in Switzerland, including four major ones. The little bell was then rung by the chairman. Most questions are discussed and voted upon separately in both chambers; only afterwards is there a joint resolution. If no agreement is reached, an arbitration commission is formed in each chamber. As a rule no arbitration is necessary. There is another inscription on the City Hall in Basel that I cannot resist quoting; it seems so typical to me of the Swiss mentality: 'Proceed well and you will be well followed,' meaning those who set a good example will be followed by the people.

The Federal Constitution of 1848 was drawn up when fear of a destructive civil war forced the cantons to tighten the bonds. The Constitution, partly revised in 1874, sustains the differences between the cantons; no unification was sought but only a mutually viable compromise.

Today Swiss politicians from all levels, languages and confessions still endeavour to achieve effective compromise. Their state has been established on a base of mutual tolerance - that is the principle respected, both in political and in everyday life. Striving to keep a balance entails a certain resistance to anything new. I give an example, not from politics: in 1848, contrary to parts of neighbouring countries, there were practically no railways in Switzerland because hoteliers, coachmen, and the rural population fought against them, fearing a loss of income.

Resistance to change also led to a certain political isolation, to an indifference towards the outside world and its problems, to a narrow and confined viewpoint. Historians and intellectuals still argue bitterly over whether Switzerland cultivates double standards: its own standards and standards for others. It was the survival instinct that compelled Switzerland to compromise with Germany and Italy in World War II by transporting goods for these countries and delivering arms to them. At the same time, though, Hermann Hesse, Thomas Mann and Bertolt Brecht were able to live and work there, as well as actors, artists, musicians, doctors and research scientists.

During World War I Hermann Hesse and Romain Rolland, who were living there, described Switzerland as an 'outstanding example for the rest of Europe', 'an island of justice and peace' which offered refuge to the 'exhausted travellers from all countries' fleeing from 'blind, unbridled violence'. In the '30s Hermann Hesse wrote to the German authorities in response to their demand for details of his racial descent: 'I refuse to sign this confirmation, not because I am no Aryan but because this demand is incompatible with the feelings and self-respect of a Swiss citizen.'

So my answer to the question whether neutrality and tolerance are always good things - by moral standards - will have to be more subtly differentiated. 'Because everything outside is wild and lawless,' wrote Friedrich Dürrenmatt, 'the Swiss feel safe from attack in their prison. They feel free, freer than other people, but they are prisoners of their neutrality.' Today Swiss politicians emphasise that every political problem in this country is turned into a moral one. God rules! Think of that quintessentially Swiss play by Max Frisch, *Biedermann and the Arsonists* (in which 'Biedermann' stands for the petty bourgeois).

Anna: Behind the house ... oh, Frau Biedermann, the sky - if you look out of the kitchen, the whole sky is on fire ...

Biedermann (pale and motionless): *Luckily it's not here ... luckily it's not here ... luckily ...'*
'Our good luck was an illusion,' emphasised Max Frisch. 'We were living very close to the torture chamber, we heard the screams of the tortured, but we were not the ones who were screaming.' This national caution has another side to it – the growing moral and political conscience of society.

I began to realise what the notorious Swiss compromise actually means when I asked a well-known television journalist in Zurich about the 'fourth power', about party membership and the interests of television, about employee politics and the influence of party interests when reporting. 'I have never belonged to a party and do not intend to, but that man over there,' he said with a glance over his shoulder, 'resigned recently from the Radical

Democratic Party (FDP). In principle we know nothing of our colleagues' party membership. For us, professionalism and knowledge of the subject are the things that matter.'

In the civil war of 1847 the liberal Protestants gained the upper hand over the conservative Catholics; they won but were, by their own account, reasonable victors. The federalism established in the Constitution of 1848 was the 'great Swiss compromise' and the Swiss government remained consistently liberal until 1891.

Towards the end of the 1950s, a coalition government was elected in which all parties were represented. The so-called 'magic formula' was 2 + 2 + 2 + 1, each of the three major parties - the Christian Democratic People's Party (CVP), the Radical Democratic Party (FDP), and the Social Democratic Party (SP) - having two seats and the remaining one going to the Swiss People's Party (SVP). All seven members of the Federal Council possess the same rights and from their midst the president of the Confederation is elected for a period of one year only; he becomes the representative of the state at public and social occasions. Should one of them resign, convention dictates that a candidate from the same party and usually from the same language region takes his place. The new councillor or minister has no idea to which department he will be assigned - the vacancy can be filled by any other minister. It is possible, for example, for a medical doctor to be appointed Minister of Defence or Foreign Affairs. The Federal Council is elected by and therefore dependent on the parliament. But the city councillors in Geneva, for example, are elected directly by the people for a period of four years, as is the mayor, and are therefore relatively independent of the parliament with its one hundred members.

Today's heated debates on professional versus volunteer (militia) politics engender three main points of view. The first: everything shall remain unchanged to avoid bureaucratic corruption and to keep members in touch with the needs and daily lives of their voters. The second: a completely professional parliament. And the third: everything shall remain unchanged but each member shall be allotted an administrative assistant or secretary who will prepare questions and documents professionally. It was this last point of view that cropped up most in my discussions with government members and journalists, who supported it with solid arguments.

But one also hears the following: members of parliament greatly overrate their importance. In fact, the propagation of politics as a hobby in Switzerland actually conceals a host of duties carried out by 'part-time' politicians. A renowned sociologist takes the view that the militia system is a very convenient myth for Swiss politicians. A 1990 investigation into the distribution of political work showed that the designation 'part-time politician' actually applied to only two per cent.

A member of the council in a large town voluntarily resigned from parliament three months ago. The main reason for his decision was a feeling of extreme frustration: 'Parliament makes no progress, it is a political word-mill. The political system is lethargic; it is organised in such a way that nothing moves.' Yes, people are free to speak and move around, but politically they are asleep as there is no real opposition which would lend a dynamic to political life. Basically the only means of manifesting opposition in Switzerland is by collecting signatures in order to introduce an initiative. Legally there are all the necessary structures: the political parties and parliament. But does it all really function? According to some of the intellectuals, the government's 'magic formula' no longer reflects reality. The world situation changes rapidly, but the government's reaction is slow. In an unstable society a 'magic formula' may be a good thing, but in a stable one it is possibly a hindrance and has a soporific effect.

Voting participation is usually very low. 'I think we are nearing the end of the system,' was the gloomy opinion of the politician who had pointedly resigned from parliament, 'as political life in its present form is absurd.'

At the meeting of the National Council that I attended, the subject of debate was exceptional: the Gulf War. But, I was assured, work would carry on as usual. Nothing must be allowed to upset parliamentary routine. One member was engrossed in his newspapers. Another was chatting casually with a neighbour, presumably a party colleague. Still another left the splendid chamber without further ado and made his way to the in-house café. Finally, exhausted by the unfamiliar calmness of the debate, I retired there too. Over a cup of coffee I asked a member why there was such indifference towards the statements of colleagues who, after all, represent the major parties of the country? Well, a great deal depends on the speaker and the subject of debate! (Women, by the way, are far more determined and interesting than their male counterparts. They were not granted the right to vote nationally until 1971. The women of French-speaking Switzerland were granted this privilege on a cantonal level between 1959 and 1961, but the more conservative Swiss-Germans did not give in until much later, after a national referendum on this 'painful' question. Women are poorly represented in parliament; today there is talk of increasing the quota to 50 per cent at all levels.) In any case, the answer to my query was accompanied by a faint smile: 'I'm afraid everything is so predictable...'

Back in the council chamber with its monumental fresco illuminated by the pale light of winter, I listened once more to the various speakers and began to understand that, whatever individual differences there may be, something had long since united them, something they had acquired during the complex history of Switzerland that lay far beyond the solemn, ponderous buildings in Berne: the original drive for survival has since been transformed into a faith in prosperity. To me, there is something constructed, something architectural about it.

Have you ever been to Zurich?

There you can see a small and elegant memorial: a house designed by the famous Le Corbusier. It stands in a public park on Lake Zurich. It seems to me no coincidence that Le Corbusier, whose ideas affected 20th century architecture worldwide, was Swiss.

The Swiss think architecturally - even in politics. Their political system is a solidly founded structural balance of political, national, social and regional interests. It functions on three levels - the commune, the canton and the Confederation. Everybody knows how many cantons there are in Switzerland but few know that there are approximately 3000 communes;

self-administrative political units with their own laws and governing bodies. The system is structured from below, just as every normal person builds his house on foundations. This firm, solid base, these fundamentals, so to speak, form the chief values in the life and politics of Switzerland.

Churwalden, where I spent about a day, is a commune of a little over a thousand inhabitants. But there are also tiny communes of only 200 inhabitants and larger ones with tens of thousands.

The local council, which as a rule consists of five members in communes the size of Churwalden, is elected every four years by popular vote. Together with its president, a fellow member of the council, it conducts the business of the commune after working hours and its members receive only a modest remuneration. Those whose families have lived in the community for centuries have the greatest influence. These people form their own citizenry within the commune. In Churwalden, for instance, they own the local forests.

One or more parties may be represented in a local governing body. There are also 'one-party communes'. But of the five members in Churwalden, two are Radical Democrats, two belong to the Swiss People's Party, and one is independent. (As a rule, Switzerland's major parties are represented in the governing bodies at the three levels of commune, canton and Confederation.) The president belongs to the Radical Democratic Party which is the strongest party in the country and was established back in the middle of the last century. For a long time it was the government party and had the absolute majority in the Federal Parliament. Nevertheless, the president does not represent party interests but the interests of his commune. The local council in Churwalden administers a budget of over two million francs a year, but may only take responsibility for sums of less than 20,000 francs. In all other cases the decisions are made at communal meetings.

Are the local councils in any way subordinate to the federal capital of Berne, I asked? The president smiled: 'We don't wish to hear anything from Berne! We are independent. We wish to be free, that is the main thing.' The commune takes the decisions on questions of schooling, road-construction and tourism. A substantial income is derived from the glittering snow and sunshine, the Rothorn peak, the wonderful skiing slopes and charming comfortable hotels in superbly restored buildings whose history goes back centuries.

Switzerland's political parties are also based in the communes. A Swiss identifies himself strongly with his commune; it is of vital importance to him. This was explained to me by the owner of a grocery in a town in the heart of Aargau, whom I met in the restaurant on top of the sunny Rothorn. He was once an active member of the Radical Democrats but had to give it up, in fact he had to resign from the party altogether, as the members of other parties no longer frequented his shop and, as you can imagine, this seriously affected his business.

How does direct democracy function in the local commune? To start an initiative among the people, a certain number of signatures is necessary. Once they have been collected, the issue is put to the vote. If the result is positive, the initiative becomes law. In this way opposition is absorbed by the Establishment before it can even arise.

Although many people find voting by a show of hands undemocratic because of pressure from relatives, neighbours or friends, foreigners are often enthusiastic about this ancient form of public ballot still practiced in Glarus, both Appenzell cantons, Obwalden and Nidwalden. The *Landsgemeinde*, as it is called, is viewed as evidence of true democracy and dates back to the Middle Ages. In fact, many participants still carry ancestral swords with them. Even Alexander Solzhenitsyn frequently expressed his delight at the meetings of the Appenzell Landsgemeinde. But for some Swiss they are a relic of the past with no democratic impact.

Communal autonomy is the building block of Swiss democracy. The communes are the bricks of which the cantons are built, and from these cantons the state is set up as a whole. The Swiss citizen has three affiliations. He is first a member of his local commune, then of the canton and lastly of the Confederation. As instruments of direct democracy, initiatives and referendums are operative – with some variations – on all three levels. The implementation of these rights is an arduous task which requires genuine Swiss patience and endurance. Forming the new Canton of Jura, formerly a part of Berne, took some forty years of meticulous work by various commissions on a cantonal and national level as well as several referendums. It illustrates a civilised solution to a minority problem. The historian J. R. von Salis aptly qualifies the character of the Swiss Confederation: 'Unity yes, uniformity no.'

The practical, sensible solution to the problem of the existence of the 'other' – in all its aspects – is a time-honoured Swiss invention. And yet, quite honestly, I did not come across much interest in the 'other'. Although every Swiss is obliged to learn a second national language at school, he does not always make use of this. At parliamentary sessions or at a meeting, at a party congress or a scientific conference each person is free to speak his mother tongue, and it is taken for granted that the other participants understand, which is mostly the case. But in coffee breaks or at lunch people form groups, more by language than by common viewpoints or interests. In the German-speaking part of Switzerland I travelled with a girl who was born in Thurgau, studied in Zurich, and had spent her vacations travelling in Italy, Germany and France but had never once been to the French-speaking part of Switzerland!

During the turbulent and bloody 20th century an elitist feeling has gained ground in the political consciousness of the Swiss: We are a chosen, an exceptional people who are not affected by the problems which tear other countries apart. There is a widespread myth which reads: Here we have created an island of freedom and law, an island of good against bad. And our boundaries are – in every sense – sacred.

Yes, in the mid-'50s, when those in power today were in the flower of youth, Switzerland really did seem to be a paradise. But now if one single boundary remains in Europe it will be a Swiss one.

Today in Switzerland the question of a united Europe is a question of freedom itself. It is slowly beginning to influence national politics, from which the Swiss basically feel alienated, particularly after the scandals caused by the so-called 'secret army' or the spying on suspect citizens and the extensive files kept on them. 'This is not our nation, it is alien to us,' say young politicians, 'and its political life is stable, which means dead – nothing is more serene than a cemetery. We are endeavouring to put some life into politics, to stir interest in political issues. We must open the windows wide and let in some air.' Those representatives of the middle generation who are dissatisfied with the conditions of political life also feel that Swiss democracy is no longer realistic: because it is so conservative, they call it, 'an ancient democracy, governed by ancient people.'

The relationship to 'others' is constantly changing. For many of the younger generation a second national language has become self-evident. Life styles have changed and mobility has increased. A young person can buy a rail pass for 400 Swiss francs that is valid all over Europe. These young people, who call themselves the 'Interrail Generation', see not only the continent but also their own country in a new light. The idea of the Swiss as an exceptional people no longer seems valid.

The question of joining Europe is the main issue of the day, particularly in view of the opening of national borders to European Community members, planned for 1 January 1993. Although young people no longer consider it all that exciting to carry a Swiss passport, they still profit from all the privileges it brings, but they would welcome the chance of the additional European citizenship.

Another paradox of the Swiss political system is that its structure has such a fine mesh that the political enthusiasm on a national level is rather diluted by the time it filters down to the people. The Swiss are not the most impassioned voters and yet two-thirds participated in the referendum on the abolition of their army, which is a very large turnout by Swiss standards. The Swiss, a young journalist told me, no longer feel they are Swiss. The people of Geneva prefer French TV to Swiss; in Zurich and Basle they watch German programmes and in Ticino it is the Italian ones. 'We are aware that we shall be living in a European community and no longer just a Swiss one,' a man from Lausanne self-confidently assured me. An older, more conservative man from Zurich was more cautious: 'We are in Europe already. The question is how much of our democracy we'll have to sacrifice. We must preserve the concept of a Swiss democracy!' The opinion of pro-European, progressive thinkers is quite different. The president of the European lobby in a city council declares: 'What we consider a traditional Swiss democracy is an anti-democracy at times.' Many farmers and manual workers are sceptical about a united Europe. Many Swiss fear an invasion of foreigners. And it is quite possible that in the event of a ballot the majority will be against Switzerland joining Europe, as they were a few years ago when three-quarters voted against Switzerland joining the UNO, even though all the parties in government and almost the whole of parliament were in favour. And yet, more than 20 per cent of all the UNO buildings and organisations are on Swiss soil – another paradox.

Yes, the 'golden egg' at the heart of Europe is in danger of cracking. For this reason there is a certain political caution toward proposals from outside. But Switzerland's powerful Big Business is on the lookout for new contacts, knowing full well that the concept of a 'pure' Switzerland will not bring in more wealth. The famous Nestlé company was established in the 19th century by political refugees from Germany, Maggi by Italians, Brown Boveri by English and German entrepreneurs. Switzerland became wealthy because it knew exactly how to make use of foreign capital and foreign labour. And the fact that today relatively young politicians are trying to integrate second-generation immigrants and take an interest in their plight demonstrates Swiss pragmatism more than it does their faith in democracy; they are fully aware of the advantages the 'second generation' will bring to a future Switzerland. The reserve toward the 'other' is a serious political problem which is rooted in the past. In order to overcome this psychological inheritance, young people in Lausanne have opened a 'bank where ideas and contacts can be exchanged with Swiss-Germans and Swiss-Italians free of charge.' There, for example, a visit to one's beloved hometown or village in the mountains can be arranged. I was told of a drive launched by an influential weekly magazine to have the universities of Switzerland give their students the opportunity to study for two semesters in another part of the country. How moved I was by this proposal to correct fears and prejudices, which surely came from the heart! Oh no, not at all, I was told. It is not the heart that dictates, but our Swiss pragmatism. For the future benefit of the country, a generation is needed which is able to work under new conditions, otherwise Switzerland will no longer be at the heart of Europe but will end up on the sidelines.

In a country where the power of the state is weak – 'weak' is not a value judgement but confirmation of the fact that the powerful state of Switzerland consciously exercises restraint – a powerful economy prevails. In my opinion it is economic growth which will ultimately determine the political future of this nation. That is why the conservatives are politically stronger today - they dominate in the political life of the country, not so much by being active in parliament but more through parliamentary committees which research a variety of problems and can, of course, often influence results.

The clockwork mechanics of Swiss democracy have some undemocratic facets. Newly-emerging political movements are quickly absorbed and their substance integrated into the larger parties. This is the fate of the women's movement, it has been so well integrated that it is in danger of disintegrating; the same applies to the ecological movement which was absorbed into the Green Party, or to the anti-nuclear movement. A striking case in point is the youth movement of 1968 whose great moments are long past. Today, the former leaders, blazing tribunes of the '60s, clearly belong to the Establishment, enthroned in their splendid law practices and financial companies.

Nationwide there are over 1200 different associations, from the horsedealers' association to the artists' association. Almost every adult in Switzerland is a member of two or three such organisations, which often wield considerable influence in parliamentary committees. This multiplicity of associations and organisations is typically Swiss but voters still elect people, not parties.

Is it the art of compromise at all levels of life that has led to the glossing over of political conflicts? Or is it indifference towards politics? The majority of people belong to the middle class and seem oblivious to conflict. A politician of the older generation would answer us proudly: of course, it is the art of compromise. Another, who not long ago rode the waves

of the student unrest, will complain of indifference. They are each right in their own way. Fear of not keeping abreast of political processes in Europe is growing and there are fewer illusions about the decorative role of the political institution. I met one family who, although quite wealthy, are dissatisfied with political life and have chosen to live on the 'fringes' of Switzerland, independent of all institutions. By engaging in no political activity at all, such drop outs use their way of life to protest against political routine; they no longer vote, they avoid both political traditions and passing trends. Compared to life, say, in Calcutta or even Moscow, they live in luxury – they have all they need, and tomorrow, if they wish, they can move into a comfortable house. Yet their unconventional way of life stems from a deep feeling of dissatisfaction, from a seething energy which has found no outlet.

I am Swiss but I do something about it is the title page of the special issue of the weekly magazine *L'Hebdo*, devoted to the 700-year jubilee. In response to the invitation of the editors to 'name three qualities which in your opinion describe Switzerland', readers under 20 wrote: 'isolated, wealthy, asleep', 'sterile, comfortable', 'lonely', 'fearful, reserved'. Asked about the ideal state of the future, the Swiss citizens of the 21st century answered: 'open (towards Europe), livelier', 'with a more open face towards Europe, more united', 'open, international, honest', 'more human, self-critical', 'open, peaceful, helping other countries', and finally, 'European, but still with its mountains.' They want to foster openness while remaining unique; they are prepared for a marked shift in political orientation but want to preserve the Swiss character. Will these young people be able to make their dreams come true? Knowing the pragmatic character of the Swiss, I am sure they will.

Question: 'What would you like to change?' Answers: 'Almost everything.' 'Hardly anything.' When I left the editorial offices of *L'Hebdo*, I mistakenly pressed the wrong button in the lift and found myself leaving the building on a different street level. The building, in which the magazine occupies one floor, is constructed on the principle of a mountain. Doesn't this apply to the country's political structure as well? It is not quite clear at first how many levels there are and how each is related to the other.

Not All the Women in This Country are Called Heidi – Women in Switzerland
Thanh-Huyen Ballmer-Cao

Remember Heidi, the girl who embodies the Swiss mountains and pastures in Johanna Spyri's book? She must be the world's most famous Swiss maiden. But the fact that she was practically the last European woman to be enfranchised and win the right to vote barely caused a ripple outside of Switzerland. After all, does Heidi, that little flower in the midst of an immaculate alpine landscape, really need to be on equal footing with Swiss men?

Well, as a matter of fact, she does. That quiet 20th-century revolution common to all western nations has indeed taken place in this mountainous country. The status and role of women have undergone changes on an unprecedented scale. Here, as elsewhere, women members of parliament give newspaper interviews, and we are starting to come across women carpenters and women pilots. Moreover, it is in this model country - in terms of prosperity and consensus - that poverty is becoming a women's issue, and that the trade unions organised a women's strike for the summer of 1991. So a lot of things have changed or are changing in Switzerland and these changes may be gradually phasing out the country's insular character.

I. In Line with Its History, Switzerland has Swum against the Tide in Its Treatment of Feminist Issues

A century and a half of waiting. 1991: The Swiss Confederation is commemorating its 700th anniversary, but at the same time a substantial portion of its population is celebrating another jubilee: 20 years of women's suffrage, introduced in 1971, a century and a half after men were given the vote.

Throughout its history, Switzerland has developed in defiance of centralised power and, we might say, of women, or at least at women's expense. As late as the end of the '60s it still looked as if nothing was going to change. While Joan Baez was mobilising the Californian campuses against the Vietnam War and the women students at the Sorbonne were calling for emancipation, participation and democratisation, the resolutely macho Swiss were still hesitant about women's suffrage. There was no shortage of speakers for and against, but on both sides people were merely reiterating the same fantasies - both unoriginal and unfounded - that had been expressed by their European neighbours decades before. 'Social degeneration' and 'the breakdown of the family' worried some people, while others entertained hopes of 'more morality in public life' and 'politics with charm and elegance'.

How federalism encouraged inequality. There was no shortage of pressure from women's organisations and initiatives in liberal political circles, but nothing ever came of it. The introduction of women's suffrage at the federal level, which implied a modification of the Swiss Constitution, had to be approved not only by the enfranchised people, but also by the cantons. This double majority rule is one of the many aspects of the Swiss political system which seek to combine democratic equality (one person, one vote) with regional parity (one canton, one vote). Thus, where major issues are concerned the least populous cantons can have their opinions ratified to the detriment of those of the larger urbanised cantons. When the first vote was taken in 1959, women's suffrage was rejected by 67 per cent of the voters and 22 of the then 25 cantons. At the second attempt in 1971, when it was finally accepted by 66 per cent of the electorate, the 'aye' was nearly converted into a 'nay' since it was rejected by eight cantons and finally approved with only a very narrow majority of four cantons. Swiss federalism therefore guarantees the cantons the power of sharing in decision-making at the federal level and at the same time sovereignty on the cantonal level. This system has the advantage of respecting the autonomy of the cantons, but also of tolerating regional disparities. The introduction of women's suffrage at the local level was a good example of this: if you had the good fortune to live in the Cantons of Geneva, Neuchâtel or Vaud, you would have won the right to vote and the right to be elected in 1959, while, if you lived in Appenzell, you would have had to wait another 30 years!

Making up for lost political time. Although they were the last in Europe to be delivered from their status as second-class citizens and to be enfranchised, Swiss women have caught up relatively quickly. They are still under-represented in the country's decision-making structures as they are everywhere else in the world, but the modest Swiss proportion of 15 per cent for women in elected posts is now slightly higher than the European average. At present the record is held by the town parliaments, where women number around 20 per cent.

This accelerated integration of women into political life is due in part to the role played by associations in Switzerland. It is hardly an exaggeration to say that you can tell Swiss men – or women – by the number of societies to which they belong. Even without the right to vote, Swiss women were integrated within an impressive network of associations, from gymnastic societies and singing clubs to unions of farming women and consumers, from countless women's church organisations to public service associations. More recently, we have seen the formation of numerous projects and networks designed to encourage mutual aid among women, and these groups are expanding rapidly. This network is instrumental in providing an enviroment in which women can hone their skills and establish the electoral basis necessary for their political activities.

Unlike some western countries, women in elected positions in Switzerland differ from their male counterparts in terms of age and education. Women deputies in Berne are, on average, just over 40, and many of them have had a university education. In contrast male politicians are on average 50 years of age and far fewer of them have a university degree.

This somewhat élitist profile of women politicians is in fact one of the residual effects of the belated introduction of women's suffrage in Switzerland. Here more than elsewhere, the conditions of access to the decision-making structures are more exacting for women than they are for men. Who could be better qualified than the women of a new generation who have enjoyed the benefits of the required socialisation and training?

A woman's world. Women living in a woman's world? This is no longer impossible, even if

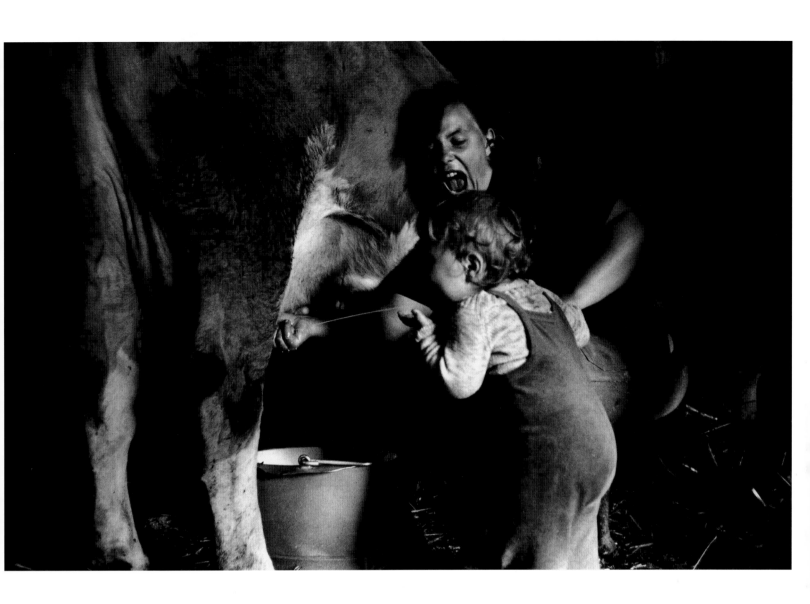

you live in Switzerland. Women are no longer forced to lead the life of an expatriate in New York or London. With a bit of research, you can find exclusively female circles in Basle and Zurich. If you wish, you can spend the day working in a women's cooperative, have your lunch in a café where the cooking is done 'by women for women' and spend the evening dancing in a women's disco or playing in a women's band. You can also extend this network by buying your books in women's bookshops, having your bicycle repaired in women's workshops and going on tours organised by women's travel agencies. Far removed from the beaten track of tourism and even from the general Swiss public, these facilities for women are usually neither prosperous nor accepted. Given that subcultures are seldom profitable, idealism has to stand in for material gains. At the moment, public opinion is still cautious. Rejection is not universal, but support depends on the nature of the activities organised in these places and on the amount of public funding that some centres are obliged to request. Scepticism is not always without foundation. Some 'new women' are growing more radical. They are moving into direct action, occupying buildings, tearing down election posters or attacking passersby at demonstrations. But these eruptions are rare. Generally speaking, these centres are very peaceful places. There are, for example, specialist women's centres that offer macramé courses and exhibitions of painting on silk, and there are others which act as information centres, where many women receive advice on matters of health, accommodation, law and childcare.

II. The Potential of the Women's Workforce

The 'miracle' of Swiss employment still leaves women at home. After rising during the '50s, the number of working women in Switzerland underwent two decades of stagnation, except for a slight increase during the '80s. The number of employed women in relation to the female population of working age amounted to 39 per cent in 1950, 51 per cent in 1960, 52 per cent in 1970, 51 per cent in 1980, and 54 per cent in 1986. Apparently the 'Appenzell syndrome' is endemic in the labour market as well, in view of the fact that numbers started rising much earlier in other OECD countries.

Although a large number of Swiss women between the ages of 20 and 50 have entered professional life, the proportion of young mothers in the labour market is lower in Switzerland than it is in most European countries. Women in Switzerland stop working outside of the home more frequently than their counterparts in Germany or France when their first child is born.

The average income of women in many industrialised countries is less than two-thirds that of men. Astonishingly, it is not in the Mediterranean countries but in Great Britain and Switzerland that wage inequalities are greatest. In addition, trade unionism is generally less widespread among women than among men. Twelve per cent of the members of the largest union, the Swiss Federation of Trade Unions are women. It would seem, then, that the group of 'working poor' also tends to be female in Switzerland. The mechanisms of equality have been implemented very slowly. Thus the Swiss government has begun to discuss a projected anti-discrimination law aimed at smoothing out the most significant inequalities. The 'miracle of Swiss employment', put to the test during the recessions of the '70s and '80s, conceals another truth. Foreigners and women have paid the price of this miracle. On the one hand, unemployment in Switzerland was 'exported' through the departure of foreign workers, whose numbers fell by around a quarter between 1975 and 1978 and, on the other hand, it was 'absorbed' by reducing the amount of women's work (from full-time to part-time, etc.).

10,000 women engineers between now and the year 2000. If you talk to a female departmental head, you are dealing with one of the five per cent of women executives in Switzerland. If you meet a female managing director or bank director, you have the good fortune to have come across one of the rare 'female success stories', which total about two per cent. As we approach the 21st century, a woman pursuing a career in the private sector is even more exceptional in Switzerland than in most western countries. Even in the medical profession, which tends in most places to include a high proportion of women, women doctors in Switzerland account for 22 per cent, as opposed to some 50 per cent in most other European countries. Private initiatives geared towards promoting women in the economy have begun to bear fruit. For instance, the group *Don't Talk, Act* is trying to increase awareness of the problem and support businesses that wish to encourage the upward mobility of their women employees. The activities of associations, most often in connection with an international network, are another type of initiative. We might, for example, cite the International Management Symposium for Women or the Swiss branch of Women's Management Development, not to mention a host of 'clubs' such as the Association of Working Women, the Soroptimists, Zonta, or the Lions.

Given the current shortage of qualified workers, is it not astonishing that the Swiss economy is only now beginning to take an interest in women's potential? For the time being, however, attitudes are hesitant and any measures taken are cautious. Discussions currently revolve around the possibilities of greater integration in the technical professions, one of the most segregated employment markets in the industrialised world. The number of women students at the two Federal Institutes of Technology will have to be increased in the near future to fill the technological gap. Restart schemes are another possibility. Thus the Federal Office of Industry and Labour (BIGA) has launched an 'offensive' to encourage the professional training and integration of women. With the same aim in mind, the Swiss National Foundation for Scientific Research has recently abandoned the age limit for students who are mothers requesting scholarships. The government has even launched a national research programme to investigate ways of implementing equality between men and women.

The challenge of restructuring the Swiss economy includes the task of redefining the world of work. The national economy needs to be given new options by mobilising the maximum amount of talent and support amongst the population. It is therefore a question, on the one hand, of giving women more opportunities for participation and promotion and, on the other hand, of giving both sexes the best opportunities for reconciling family and professional responsibilities.

The economy can no longer afford to ignore the human capital of the majority of the population. In this respect, Switzerland is no different from any other country.

III. Ways of Life: When the Traditional Family is No Longer the Only Sanctuary

Over the past few decades, Switzerland has undergone profound changes in the structure of its domestic and family life. There has been a rapid increase in the number of single people as well as unmarried and childless couples. These tendencies have in the meantime become 'trans-national' and statistical differences among industrialised nations are negligible. Moreover, the process of individualisation, common to all western societies, is also affecting the sense of identity in Switzerland.

New family and domestic structures. Over a period of 20 years, between 1960 and 1980, the size of the average Swiss household shrunk by 25 per cent from 3.3 people in 1960 to 2.5 in 1980. These figures are only one indication of a profound break with traditional ways of life. While the family unit consisting of a married couple and two children is certainly not about to disappear, it does not represent an exclusive model of cohabitation. More and more young people are choosing to remain single. A survey in Zurich showed that barely half of the city's inhabitants between the ages of 22 and 29 have the firm intention of getting married. An increasing number of young women are no longer prone to consider single life as a temporary state. From being a passing phase, it is gradually becoming institutionalised as a permanent way of life. In addition, if young Swiss women get married, they not only do so later than their mothers did, but also wait longer before having children.

Polls show that Swiss women prefer a family of two children, French women express the wish to have three children. At present, the birth rate is around 1.5 per Swiss woman of childbearing age. In addition, given that a third of couples are childless, the tendency not to have any children seems more widespread in Switzerland than in France or Italy. Does Switzerland run the risk of becoming a childless society sooner than its neighbours? Whatever the answer, when Swiss men and women decide to have children, they prefer to do so within well-defined legal frameworks. The rate of extra-marital births is, in fact, lower in Switzerland than in Denmark or Germany.

But, beware, a distinction should be drawn between these statistics which show a world populated by individualists and the everyday world informed with family values. Despite the increase in the number of divorces, single-parent families – four-fifths of which consist of mothers and children – and working women, the fiscal, educational and social security systems still favour the traditional distribution of roles. Thus the legal system does not allow for separate taxation or individual pensions and most school timetables ignore the demands of working mothers. Furthermore, we should not forget the inadequate provision of child-care facilities.

Changing attitudes. Thirty-five and unmarried? Today that is no longer tantamount to being an 'old maid' or an 'old bachelor'. If you attend an official dinner alone or with a companion, you no longer risk shocking the other guests. With the rapid increase in the number of people either living alone or cohabiting outside marriage, these two ways of life have gained in popularity. As little as ten years ago, the population was reticent in its treatment of 'unconventional' ways of life. But as we enter the '90s people are starting to take them for granted and public opinion has clearly become more receptive. Currently, out of every five Swiss citizens, two consider single life to be quite acceptable and three approve of cohabitation outside marriage.

However, the climate of tolerance certainly does not entail a decline in the popularity of marriage. On the contrary, for many unmarried couples cohabitation amounts to a 'trial marriage' both in terms of the intention expressed by the people concerned and of the average duration of their cohabitation, which is less than five years. What has changed is the fact that the preference for one way of life no longer necessarily indicates the rejection or condemnation of other forms of shared living. At a very slow pace, and with occasional setbacks, Swiss attitudes are, for good or ill, following the faster rhythms of individualisation in a postmodern society.

IV. The Eternally Feminine vs. Staunch Helvetia

The image of woman, the source. We should not forget that Helvetia, a woman, represents the state of Switzerland, and she is obviously not the only woman to hold such an office; she shares the privilege with many colleagues, for instance, Marianne, Britannia and Germania. And did she not win the honour by beating the male competition, William Tell? This victory only increases her merit. Apparently a woman is better at representing things: with her 'charm and elegance', she intrinsically suggests love of family and fatherland. But beyond the advantages brought by the fantasy images of her sex, Helvetia's name possesses considerable advantages, since Helvetia's name can be pronounced without any difficulty in four national languages, her image has been elegantly integrated within the country's three cultures. And so for almost two centuries this sturdy Swiss woman, sword in hand, has watched over the Confederation and its armed neutrality. Her image also graces postage stamps and coins, and she has given her name to boulevards and town squares.

But it would be a mistake to deduce from this that the Swiss want to break forever with the idea of the Eternally Feminine. In more serious matters, for example in elections, 'Mother Courage'-type combatants from the Women's Liberation Movement (WLM) fare badly. The electorate still tends to favour candidates whose image connotes the values held to be 'feminine' – motherhood, altruism and practicality.

Helvetia certainly has no monopoly on representation. There are other women celebrities who are the pride of the nation. 'Viscerally republican' Switzerland is not only anti-royalist, but also resolutely anti-hero. Suspicious of all forms of leadership, sceptical of excessive cleverness, this country fiercely cultivates its distaste for personal power. But living as we do in the age of media, it is hard for the nationalist libido to do without the 'star system'. Without doubt, many people are sorry that the Swiss football team has never played in the World Cup Final. Certainly, many of them grieve that Swiss tennis-players have not enjoyed any real success. But why weep? After all, do they not get their revenge every winter the minute the snow starts to fall? Heidi Zurbriggen, Maria Walliser and Chantal Bournissen stir plenty of hearts with their regular high placings. The other 'darlings of the nation' include women figure skaters, astrologers and television announcers. Not to mention the names of other women, not so well known but illustrious none the less, such as Meret Oppenheim, Maria Becker and Anne Cuneo, who have done the honours for Swiss art, theatre and literature.

The market in solitude. 1990: three quarters of a million adults live alone, most of them women. What a potential for the trade in partnerships! In Switzerland as elsewhere, the problem is not simply the number of people in search of a soul mate, but also and more particularly the discrepancy in number between the two sexes. Women, 52 per cent of the population, live on average seven years longer than men. The ages and, often, social groups clearly diverge. In fact, along with discretion and respectability, marriage bureaux have begun to offer a special membership price to encourage men.

In the personal columns, traditional values always predominate. On the demand side, mature men who are 'cultured, active and generous', and, of course, 'in a good professional position', seek young 'dream creatures', 'sexy but feminine', in most cases with 'long hair and beautiful eyes'. On the supply side, the same 'surplus categories' are in the majority: women over 30, in most cases, cultivated, well-educated professionals and widows over 50. Interestingly enough, exacting requirements are not necessarily the exclusive domain of male advertisers. It is no longer enough for Prince Charming to have a brain and a heart. He now needs a good physique as well. The catalogue of desired attributes includes data concerning height ('at least 5ft 8in'), build ('athletic') and appearance ('neat'). The time may not yet be ripe for equality where division of labour in housework is concerned, but partnership has certainly come into its own in sharing leisure hours. Men are still looking for companions to take to dances and candle-lit dinners, but they also want soul mates with whom to share their tastes ('Vivaldi and Picasso') and their hobbies ('squash and skiing', or 'rambles in the country-side').

V. And Foreign Women?

They are a constant presence. They wait on you in restaurants, they sit at the cash register in supermarkets. The Swiss banks would never be so tidy or the universities so clean without them. Although a large number of them work, the foreign women who live in Switzerland have a very low profile. To a certain extent they are the country's hidden continent.

Multicultural society for women. As the global village becomes reality, multicultural Swiss society is becoming increasingly multi-ethnic. The four languages and the two religions have more than quadrupled in recent years. The Limmat valley in Zurich already encompasses 40 nationalities. The conurbation of Geneva must have even more. Accounting for around 15 per cent of the resident Swiss population, the foreign population is made up almost equally of men and women. The women that you see early in the morning in trams and buses with children half asleep on their knees are very often Teresas, Giuseppinas and Rezas on their way to the crèche and to work. At 70 per cent, the rate of work among the foreign female population, which has remained constant over the past decade, is higher than that of Swiss women, for practically all age levels. In most cases these women work for 'economic' reasons, are less likely to interrupt their jobs when they have children, and in most cases do jobs referred to as 'women's work', work that is unskilled and badly paid. Little is known about their living conditions, but more and more of them are becoming clients of the social and counselling services.

There are certainly exceptions. There are famous foreign women as well: the first women to receive university degrees and the first women doctors were not Swiss. But the past bears little resemblance to the present, even less to the future. With a surplus birth rate of 56 per cent, are foreign women not the 'fountain of youth' in an ageing Switzerland? For two decades the number of Swiss children brought into the world has not kept pace with the preceding generations. In the immediate future, the naturalisation policy currently in force, one of the most restrictive in the world, provides no solutions. Young people who are born and/or educated in Switzerland, but are the children of foreign immigrant parents, are not automatically naturalised, but are eligible only for a fast-track naturalisation procedure. Therefore, any demographic option other than a decline in population depends partly on the way in which Swiss society deals with the integration of this part of the population.

Exotic, erotic and faithful: the trade in women. 'Swiss man seeks Swiss woman.' This personal advertisement, which one might normally have expected to be successful, could easily fail. More likely than not, it comes from a category of marriage candidates who have had singularly bad luck in Switzerland. They are basically the young farmers from the mountain regions, mature men - often of modest means - hoping for wives their daughters' age, men in search of women who, as in the good old days, 'don't need to constantly assert themselves'. For these men, Swiss women are, for once, 'too emancipated'. So they prefer to recruit elsewhere, preferably in Asia or the islands of the Indian Ocean. For years specialist tours have enabled Swiss clients to make a personal selection of what we must regrettably refer to as 'merchandise'. For those who prefer to do their shopping from home, there are special catalogues which provide detailed data with photographs and also a guarantee of return if the choice does not prove to be 'satisfactory'.

Certainly, these Filipino or Thai women do not always end up in massage parlours or bars and nightclubs of dubious repute. The men who have married them do not see them as slaves. There may even be some success stories. But many of these women are faced with a life of sexual and economic abuse, and all of them suffer to a greater or lesser extent from human and social isolation. Madness and suicide often wreak havoc among them. On the other hand, female solidarity is assuming a more concrete form: Swiss women are no longer content to denounce the trade in Third World women, but are now trying to offer specific help through counselling services, support networks and solidarity organisations.

When will Switzerland stop being an island? Stability has long been the key to Switzerland's success. But is the formula a timeless one? Can Switzerland remain motionless while the world moves around it? Will Switzerland look on passively while the future is being built next door? The status of women is without a doubt one of the areas in which society is changing most rapidly, and Switzerland, at the age of 700, realises this but is still too timid to get on the bandwagon.

Exoticism is appealing, but having something in common is what brings people together. If you appreciate the distinctive characteristics of Swiss society, you, too, can do your part in making it easier for Switzerland to share the features that she has in common with other peoples. In all probability, you will see Switzerland with different eyes the next time you stay in this country. Of course, Heidi will still smile at you from the boxes of Suchard chocolates and Caran d'ache crayons, but maybe you'll get to know Paula, the young ecology student who will be your guide, or exchange a few words with Marthe, the pensioner who runs the kiosk by the entrance to the museum. Only then will you realise that Heidi has come down from the mountains.

The Arrow and the Apple – A Letter from Switzerland

Ali Salem

I

Switzerland is the perfect example of a country whose essential unity lies in the diversity of its parts, or in the homogeneity of its differences - Cantons, Catholics and Protestants, the French, Swiss German, Italian and Romansh languages, all coexist peacefully and they have never hesitated to admit that nothing would be more ridiculous than to try suppressing the differences that exist in each other.

Switzerland has opted for a policy of 'neutrality'. Of course without the agreement of the international community this would carry no weight at all – but it must be remembered that this agreement has saved the country from the catastrophic consequences of two world wars. Then again, what has Switzerland got to offer invaders? There are practically no raw materials. The beauty of the landscape or the precision of its inhabitants? For invaders the first trump card would be meaningless and the second an actual handicap to occupation, as the inhabitants have a historically authenticated reputation for being brave fighters, capable of splitting opponents' skulls with a single blow of an axe. In return for being left in peace, Switzerland offers an excellent corridor between northern and southern Europe, the chance of a wonderful summer holiday, and a safe deposit box in which to keep legally (or illegally) acquired assets.

This attitude has a long history and is closely connected to the question: what made the Swiss Swiss? A difficult question that I have thus far not even been able to answer for my own country either: what made the Egyptians Egyptian?

Do you remember the episode of William Tell, who refused to salute the Hapsburg Bailiff Gessler's hat on a pole, with the result that Gessler sentenced him to shoot an apple from his son Walter's head with an arrow? People all over the world have their own myths and legends in which despots compel heroes to perform courageous deeds, but why do the Swiss, especially the German-speaking Swiss, always turn to this particular episode? Far more important than whether the hero Tell ever really lived is the message hidden behind these legends that are said to have occurred so many centuries ago. The struggle between good and evil? Gessler as a dictator and Tell as a free man who refuses to bow to authority? I don't see anything particularly new in that. Many Swiss men and women I spoke to see this incident as a symbol of Swiss pride and the struggle against tyranny. But this still does not give me an answer to the question of how the legend has managed to survive for so long.

I believe its message goes well beyond the eternal struggle between freedom and dictatorship. I think that the episode is above all about William Tell's fear: the moment of nervous tension when he aimed at the apple on his son's head. It is precisely there that the decisive climax of the episode lies – the rest is inessential.

The message is clear. Aim straight! Be skilful! Be precise! Past experience is irrelevant; now you must rely on your skill alone. Aim with a steady hand! Your first mistake will be your last. You will have no chance of rectifying it. You must hit your target or lose everything that is dear to you!

So freedom is associated with a job done well; liberation depends on zeal, on commitment. Perfection is the only way to escape subjugation. Every Swiss holds a weapon in his hand and aims at an imaginary apple, driven by fear and nervous tension. And the fact that William Tell did not carry any old weapon, but a crossbow, a weapon in the shape of a cross, gives the episode an additional religious dimension.

Laughter would be out of place at the moment of nervous tension as the arrow flies towards the apple. I must also add that in earlier times the Swiss had to seem serious and staunch if they wanted to be engaged as professional fighters, mercenaries in the service of other nations. After all, who would hire a soldier with a grin on his face?

II

And today, as a new order dawns in Europe, will Switzerland remain neutral? What will the country gain, what can it expect if it continues to pursue this policy? What price has Switzerland already paid, and what will it have to pay in future?

The great Swiss dramatist and writer Friedrich Dürrenmatt gave a possible answer before a large audience. When his fellow writer, Czechoslovakian president Vaclav Havel, was awarded a prize in Switzerland, Dürrenmatt addressed the prizewinner, saying, 'We are giving you a peace prize, but we live in a big prison ourselves.' It is hardly necessary to describe the effect this statement had on the audience. A woman friend who was present told me: 'The dignitiaries rose from their seats, expressing impatience, mixed with nervousness. One of them whispered in my ear and asked me how this man could dare make such an outrageous statement.'

But what did Dürrenmatt say? Here is an extract from the now famous speech: 'Man makes everything paradoxical, reason becomes unreason, justice injustice, freedom unfreedom, because man himself is a paradox, an irrational rationality. Like your tragic grotesques, Switzerland might also be seen as a grotesque: as a prison - admittedly very different from the prisons you were thrown into, my dear Havel - into which the Swiss have escaped. Because lawlessness reigns outside the prison and because they are only secure against attack inside the prison, the Swiss feel free, freer than other people. They are free as prisoners in the prison of their neutrality. There is just one difficulty with this prison, and that is the difficulty of proving that it is not a prison but a bulwark of liberty, because seen from the outside, a prison is a prison and its inmates are prisoners, and if they are prisoners, then they are not free. Seen from the outside, only the warders count as free, because if they were not free, they would of course be prisoners. To solve this contradiction the prisoners introduced compulsory guard duty: every prisoner proves his freedom by being his own warder. Thus a Swiss has the dialectical advantage of being free, and both a prisoner and a warder. The prison does not need walls, because its prisoners are warders and guard themselves, and because the warders are free men, they do business among themselves and with the whole world, and how! and, on the other hand, because they are prisoners, they cannot join the United Nations and they are worried about the European Economic Community.'

The essence of Dürrenmatt's statement is that in our day the idea of neutrality has become

irrational, and that the walls we build for our protection are ultimately those that shut us in. Dürrenmatt's words conclude in love and hate. Actually, it is almost the duty of a writer to resort to shock treatment in order to jolt the people and the state, the way someone might be jolted by a heart attack. Dürrenmatt died in 1990, but his words live on. My friend told me that those members of the audience who expressed displeasure had to admit that Dürren-matt had in fact spoken very well, and was a great man. All I can say to that is: that is only natural. The powerful man says to the artist: die or stop being creative, so that I can make a speech in your praise.

The country's other great writer, Max Frisch, who was ten years his senior and died in 1991, also spent a lifetime studying his native land. I recall a scene from his play *Graf Oederland*. The protagonists of the play are the public prosecutor, to whom a strange case is passed, and the accused, an honest cashier at a bank, conscientious and with an impeccable repu-tation, never absent without reason and always punctual; an exemplary employee. A man without vices. One evening he suddenly leaves home, goes to the bank, and kills the care-taker with an axe. This is what he says to his defence counsel by way of explanation:

Doctor Hahn: *I will recapitulate. On Sunday afternoon you went to the football international, you were depressed when our team lost, you went to the cinema in the evening, but the film did not hold you. You walked home and according to the records you didn't feel at all unwell.*

Murderer: *Only bored.*

Yes, weariness, a feeling you've had enough! This morbid but human desire to escape from the everday world, to break the vice-like grip of discipline. The public prosecutor suffers from depression himself. He dreams of escaping from the constraints brought by his work and the hundreds of dossiers that pile up in his office. He too is looking for the right to change, or some hope that he could, no matter where this might lead. One night his maid is lighting the fire and senses his mood of depression, boredom, discouragement, revulsion. The following scene occurs:

Hilde: *Why don't you burn it, sir, burn all that paper that you have to read all the time as public prosecutor?*

Public Prosecutor: *Burn it?*

Hilde: *That's what I'd do.*

Public Prosecutor: *You're talking like a child.*

Hilde: *That's what I'd do.*

Public Prosecutor: *Do it then.*

Hilde: *I will.*

She throws one bundle of documents into the fire, then a second, and finally all the rest, and they blaze up until the whole room is aglow and the curtain slowly closes on this wonderful scene.

This play by Frisch shows clearly how far a person is prepared to go to escape from the dread-ful vice-like grip of our age by throwing laws and instructions into the fire.

A few years ago I had an opportunity to meet Max Frisch at the Swiss cultural attaché's home in Cairo, and he admitted to me that he was also particularly fond of this scene. He had dis-

covered, he told me in a moment of enthusiasm, that in Switzerland everything was beautiful, perfect, tidy, disciplined and serious; there was no room for mistakes. He started worrying about the fate of the country. He had become aware that with this attitude no human progress was possible, and that had driven him to write the play.

Strange, I replied, because what drives us in the Third World to creativity is diametrically the opposite. We are surrounded by a lack of discipline and our mistakes are flouted in front of us. These are the things that we consider to be a hindrance to human progress.

III

I have tried to convey an impression of the image that Dürrenmatt and Frisch have created of Switzerland. I should like now to describe my own impressions, even though I can hardly achieve what these two great authors have in writing about their country.

After staying in various towns and parts of the country for a while, I also spent some time in the unique and friendly atmosphere of a little village in the midst of the Alps. I took a cable car – for the first time in my life – to the top of a mountain called the Rothorn. On the summit I felt as though I was in a great white temple. I saw the trip up there as a kind of ritual. Perhaps I was not the only one who felt like that. As a rule you find a young couple embracing each other at every tourist spot. But in the mountains I did not come across anything like that, because such places demand a certain degree of respect, and you feel as though you're somewhere near heaven and not on earth. I wonder how the Alps affect the Swiss. These expanses of white that fade into the horizon at an infinite distance must be where the concept of purity starts for the Swiss. On the other hand, life in the mountains also requires a certain discipline, indeed absolute care, as a mistake or simple negligence in the maintenance of this aerial transport system could cause a catastrophe and transform these beautiful mountains into a graveyard.

Let me describe another, but no less striking experience I had of the mountains. It was at the theatre in Buochs in central Switzerland, in a recently renovated hall without a single empty seat. I was amazed by the age of the audience; they were all over 60. Not a single young person among them. The play was set in the mountains, a long time ago. The realistic stage sets, which had to be changed between each scene, took an inordinate amount of time. The spectators had to put up with lengthy pauses and the director's main problem seemed to be how to get from one scene to the next. Watching the audience I was struck by the pleasure with which people followed the sequence of scenes. What they saw on the stage was obviously exactly what they wanted to see.

The plot required reconstruction of a past age, accurate in every detail: an old Swiss cottage, a kitchen, a bedroom, etc. The tools on stage were exactly like the ones their ancestors must have used. It was as if a museum had been transported into the theatre. The play was appropriate to the needs of a whole generation who delight in stories of their past.

But where were the young people? In Aarau I saw the writer and cabaret artist Franz Hohler in his one-man show. The audience was made up of young people. They laughed uproariously at all of his punch lines. There was no-one there over 50. The audience was always particularly amused when their government was the target of ridicule. When we laugh at the present we are at the same time destroying part of the past. Laughter, that unique substitute for violence, is a way of shaping the future or at least looking at it hopefully. Thus there is a whole generation in Switzerland that still believes in the old days and finds it important to keep memories of them alive. But there is another generation that dreams of change. At least that was the impression I got when talking to some young people in a grammar school in the Zurich country side. They all voiced the same opinion, without exception, that the Swiss have no right to think of themselves as anything special.

On the other hand, everything new requires a solid basis in the past as well. In various places in Switzerland I felt I was in Europe, in that cold ambience that I know well from other countries. But I also went to places where I sensed a different atmosphere: there I thought I was seeing real Swiss people, people who lived in the mountains, with broad shoulders that suggested hard, strenuous labour. Sitting together at a long table in a restaurant in Altdorf after the cattle market, eating and drinking, only speaking occasionally, pulling at their pipes and wearing their traditional clothes, they really did look as though they had stepped out of an old picture.

IV

Life in the mountains has been a source of inspiration for a great many Swiss artists as well. I have seen several documentary films by Fredi M. Murer; they made the life of the mountain population accessible to me. I have also seen his feature film *Höhenfeuer*, which tells the story of a father, a mother, a daughter and a deaf-and-dumb son. They live in a remote mountain farmhouse in the heart of the Alps. An incestuous relationship develops between the son and the daughter, almost inevitable in the relentless isolation. When the father discovers the relationship he loses his head and wants to shoot his son. The mother stands between them to protect him, but a shot is fired and kills her. The son joins in the struggle in an effort to end the conflict, but another shot kills the father. At the end of a slow take, a scene that is more like a ritual, daughter and son bury their parents under the snow. End of film.

A work of art can exist for art's sake, but in this case the film is trying to make a specific statement. Fredi M. Murer is one of those film makers that can be compared with painters. Every scene is transformed - even if it is quite insignificant - into an impressive tableau. I have seen how Murer draws every scene first, very precisely, attending to all the details the spectator is intended to pick up afterwards.

Why do mother and father have to die and the children survive? What will happen to them? Is the author suggesting that they have no faults, and therefore escape punishment? I am speaking of measures imposed on the hero of a tragedy, rather than of morality. Murer told me in a conversation that this incident really did happen and that a man of the mountains had told him about it. Nevertheless, it is not the task of art to copy life. In art there is another life, in which we place the aims and deeds of heroes in the context of our notions of life.

I could imagine a different ending that would make this 'good' film into an 'excellent' one: the girl and boy leave the mountains and reach the main road. They hitch-hike, travelling in oppo-

site directions to lose themselves somewhere among the inhabitants of the cities. The white mountains must remain pure. It is the cities that contain all types of individuals.

Let us leave Fredi M. Murer and look at another film maker who treats Switzerland's present and future in his own way: Rolf Lyssy's film *The Swiss Makers* caught the country's imagination a few years ago and was a great success.

The story is about a man who has filled in the necessary applications and gone through the formalities in order to become a Swiss citizen. Amusing and unexpected events include questioning by the police, who ask him about his and his wife's private life. The procedure ends with the police officer joining them for a meal and making certain that the wife really can cook a fondue (a traditional cheese dish): the sign of a good citizen.

In the course of a protracted final cross-examination which consists of singularly absurd questions the man is asked: 'What do you think William Tell would do if he were alive today?' He replies: 'Tell would kill Gessler. Because if there is a Tell, there must be a Gessler.' His answer goes down well and he is granted Swiss citizenship. A foreign dancer does not get it, but steals the heart of the policeman who is keeping her under surveillance. Finally the two decide to emigrate. But where is one to go from Switzerland? Where in the world can one emigrate, in a contemporary world where the police control every millimetre of the planet? To me, Lyssy's rendition of police oppression is little more than an innocent joke.

Nonetheless, *The Swiss Makers* is a film that expresses anger about current conditions and transforms this anger into laughter in an effort to produce a new and better future for the country.

V

When I was in Geneva I was confronted with a view of 'frontiers' that was new to me. What we in the Third World perceive as a frontier is quite different from what the word means to people here. For us it is a distant and unsettling place: the desert, getting lost, boredom, the faces and behaviour of the frontier officials. In Geneva I had breakfast in a building on the frontier. It must be pleasant to live in a house in Switzerland and be able to reach over and touch trees on French soil.

In Berne I felt uncomfortable for the first time. I visited the parliament building. In its immediate vicinity I was struck by a boy and a girl who seemed to be flirting. Then I saw, to my surprise, that the boy was holding the girl's arm and giving her an injection. Then I chanced to pass by a large rubbish bin in which I saw a heap of empty ampoules and used hypodermic syringes. For the first time in my life I was present at such a scene - in real life, not in the cinema. Filled with a sense of intense unease, I had to leave the place immediately. Why have these young people chosen to congregate at such a profoundly symbolic site? Is it a desire, conscious or unconscious, to defy the authority of the state?

Later I noticed a group of young people in Zurich rushing out of a park near the National Museum and crowding around someone who had just got out of his car. I was told he was a drug dealer. That was why the young people were in such a hurry. They had been waiting for their fix for a long time.

It is regrettable that a considerable number of young people, angry and desperate, fall under the influence of drugs amidst the riches of this country. And I think that the next few years will see Switzerland fighting a real war against drugs.

VI

Switzerland's political neutrality is reflected in the behaviour of its inhabitants; it causes indifference. I am talking about the kind of indifference in which hearts are filled with ice instead of warm blood. This sensation is combined with a feeling of superiority, but also with fear of others: 'They envy me, they envy my situation, my wealth and my well-being. I must protect myself against them.'

People are constantly trying to get away from things thought to be bad, thought to weaken the muscles of responsibility in the human nervous system. The only means of coping with life is to confront evil and take part in the struggle for its removal. It is only in this way that our life becomes real. Then we are no longer the prisoners of our ideas. It is necessary for the cruel Gessler to exist, so that the good and courageous William Tell can defeat him. It is also necessary for Gessler to appear clearly and distinctly in front of us, otherwise he would operate in twilight and perhaps win without our noticing . . .

Certain revelations made it clear to the citizens of Switzerland that a secret police exist in their country – Dürrenmatt also spoke of them, shadowing and reporting on them. This reality woke a lot of people from their angelic sleep. They discovered that their country is no longer different from any other.

Secret police, secret army? And all this in a country of freedom, and lightheartedness. Two blows that shook the people of Switzerland. The first cracks in the time-honoured legend of uniqueness and superiority.

A new generation is growing up that is re-examining the ideas and old-established facts of the country. Bitter reality has surfaced: 'Beautiful Switzerland is firmly entrenched in this dreadful world. Unspoiled Switzerland is firmly entrenched in this wretched world. Happy Switzerland is firmly entrenched in this sad world. Let us stop cultivating illusions. Let us accept our share of the "bad", like every other country in the world. Only in this way can we be free.'

An old question comes to mind: would you like to be Swiss? My answer is still 'yes', but under one simple condition. I should like to work in the Swiss Embassy in Cairo as soon as I am granted Swiss citizenship. With this nationality I would enjoy every advantage in terms of human rights. And in return - living in Cairo - I would be involved in that measure of chaos and sorrow without which life is not worth living.

VII

In his speech, Dürrenmatt said: 'Yes, we're proud of our direct democracy; yes, we have pensions for widows and orphans and the elderly; we've even amazed the world by granting women the right to vote, and we're insured against death, illness, accident, burglary and fire: happy is the man whose house burns down. Here too, politics has forsaken ideology for economics; its issues are economic issues. Where may the state intervene, where not, what should and what shouldn't be subsidized, what should and what shouldn't be taxed? Wages and leisure time are settled by negotiation. Peace is more of a threat to us than war. A harsh sentence but not a cynical one. Our roads are battlefields, our atmosphere filled with poison gases, our oceans are puddles of oil, our fields contaminated with pesticides, the Third World has been plundered worse than the Orient once was by the crusaders: no wonder that it is blackmailing us now. Not war, but peace is the father of all things; war springs from our failure to cope with peace. Peace is the problem that we have to solve.'

My dear Dürrenmatt, may God have mercy on your soul. You complain that political ideas have had to give way to economic issues? That is exactly what we need here. We are hungry and we are fed with political ideas. Nothing but political ideas to stuff men's brains with day after day. Even the fields are full of political ideas and so are newspapers, books, songs, music, theatre, television, radio, windows, doors, streets, deserts, valleys and yes, even weapons.

Nevertheless, my dear Dürrenmatt, I understand the reasons for your rage and suffering very well. You are a great artist. Many works start with suffering, then we look to see where that suffering comes from. I imagine you in paradise now, complaining about the absence or presence of certain things.

I am certain that your people have good reason to teach us about federalism and the unity of the nation. What are the indispensable prerequisites of unity? How can elements that are entirely different from each other have common aims? You sell us medicines, weapons, in brief, everything. Why do you not sell us the idea of unity? Why do you not talk about it? Explain it to us ceaselessly, for years, over and over again. In that way you could do a service to the inhabitants of the Near East, indeed of the whole world.

VIII

I am convinced that the best way to recognise the soul of a people is from the anecdotes they tell. One Swiss anecdote I heard is this: a Swiss man asks God to create a beautiful country and wonderful landscape for him. God gets to work and creates Switzerland. After he has completed his work he sits down, tired, and asks the Swiss for a bowl of milk. Before going on his way again he says to the man: 'Right, I've created what you asked for. Do you need anything else?' The Swiss promptly replies: 'Two francs for the bowl of milk, please.'

I have already mentioned how the country's tradition of neutrality has made its people emotionally neutral. Three weeks in a country naturally do not give one the right to decide whether its people's hearts contain glaciers or glowing coals. But I still cannot help wondering whether people who are in love in Switzerland count petals too and what they say to each other while doing it.

During my stay I kept asking myself what I, as an Egyptian, was supposed to think about affluent Swiss society. It is not important whether one is rich. The crucial thing is to be aware of this wealth. One can be rich and still be afraid of misery and the poor. It seems to me that this is the case with the Swiss. They seem to be saying to themselves: 'Why should I pay?

My expenses only bring me a bit closer to misery. I will pay only if I am forced to. Forget about what God has given me. I charge him for the bowl of milk because the two francs will be added to my fortune and contribute to protecting me from misery.'

I never got enough to eat in Swiss restaurants. Sometimes I even had the feeling that a single cow was doled out once a month to be divided among all the restaurants in whatever town I happened to be. Finally I discovered that many restaurants cater especially to tourists, in other words, strangers. So when I was in Lugano, I decided to inquire about a restaurant that is not frequented by tourists. That day I had enough to eat.

One of the surprising aspects of my stay in Switzerland was that many people with whom I met in restaurants did not pay the bill, or even offer to. Our oriental generosity seems to be unknown here. I assume people work on the principle: 'This man is a guest of the Swiss government and that government collects taxes from us. Therefore this is an opportunity to make it pay the guest's bill, and my own.'

A historian I visited offered us nothing at all. He seemed to take the view that he had something to say about the history of Switzerland and that was all he had been asked to do. He could easily have said, 'I should like to offer you coffee, but as you see I'm on my own here.' I thought perhaps there was not a kitchen in the building, but then I saw one on my way out.

Emil Steinberger, the cabaret artist, was very hospitable. It may well be that he is the exception that proves the rule. He treated me to several rounds of coffee and cake. We passed a pleasant few hours talking about art and theatre. And at the end he insisted on settling the bill.

Perhaps the Swiss are more generous with each other. In general - at least in their dealings with strangers - this does not seem to be the case.

IX

A few hours before my flight back to Cairo I took a final walk through Zurich, the largest city in Switzerland. And there I discovered something astonishing: a large poster with lettering on it and a lovely drawing of cats and dogs. At first I thought it was advertising an animal show. When I looked at it more closely the poster turned out to be a campaign by an insurance company that insures household pets against accidents, illness and death.

In fact, after people in Switzerland have been insured against every possible danger, the insurance company probably realised that an essential sector had been overlooked: the well-being of pets! Imagine your cat dies. You are upset about this and need compensation, a sum of money that eases the pain. You could even use the money to buy a new pet. In fact the first idea that came to me as an inhabitant of the Third World was: how do the insurance people make sure that they are not being swindled? To what extent do they trust someone who says his cat disappeared two days ago, his dog cannot bark any more, or his dog died on a mountain hike and had to be buried there and then?

I do not mind admitting to my oriental cunning. Swiss citizens obviously have better things to do than figure out ways of snapping up a few thousand francs in this country of 1001 banks.

X

I shall permit myself to end my report here. There is a richness in this country of which many people are unaware. A profound fear of poverty has taken possession of a large number of them. Everywhere in the country and in every one of their gestures you recognize a Tell challenging a Gessler, neither of whom succeeds in defeating the other. But isn't this conflict of forces intrinsic to human nature and therefore universal? Yes, but in the case of Switzerland and its inhabitants such weaknesses seem particularly blatant to us; for the simple and also very human reason that we are pleased to find faults in the very people who think themselves so faultless. In other words, this may all be nothing but the expression of a certain feeling of envy.

I have the impression that it must have been a crafty little customer who sent me the invitation to Switzerland. Have you ever tried owning only a single shirt and then being asked to look at a film star's wardrobe? Have you ever tried being hungry and then being invited to visit an expert in gastronomy, but only to inspect the kitchen? Have you ever imagined being in prison, going out into the yard to watch a film about freedom, and then being shut up in your cell again? This was my experience on my visit to this rich country.

Prosperity and Challenge in the Swiss Economy
Michael J. Enright

To many, Switzerland must seem like an economic paradise. The performance of the Swiss economy over the past four decades has been nothing short of remarkable. Per capita income and net wages are among the world's highest, while income taxes are relatively low. Labour relations have been harmonious for more than fifty years. Inflation has been low and unemployment almost nonexistent. Large current account surpluses have become routine. The Swiss Government, through stable macroeconomic policies and limited government expenditures, has helped create a climate in which firms of all shapes and sizes can prosper. And they have prospered, Swiss companies have world-leading positions in a wide range of industries. The result has been a remarkably diverse economy in which firms compete on the basis of quality and innovation. All this has been achieved without creating many of the problems found in other nations. The environment remains relatively pristine; the cities remain pleasant and human in scale.

Why then are so many in Switzerland voicing concerns about the nation's economic future? Why do some doubt that the nation's economic success will continue unabated into the next century? To answer these questions, we must first understand that there are two sides to the Swiss economy. The first is well-known to outsiders. This side is remarkably pragmatic, open and dynamic. It can be seen in a diverse range of internationally competitive industries driven by innovation and a commitment to quality. The second side is less well-known to outsiders. This side is less flexible, rather closed and relatively stagnant. It can be seen in parts of the domestic economy that are subsidised, protected or cartelised. The two sides of the Swiss economy are reflective of a deeper duality in the national psyche. Switzerland is a valley nation that looks both outward and inward. There is a desire to create and build and a desire to protect and preserve. There is a tendency toward investment and a tendency toward caution. The balance that emerges between the two sides of the economy, and the forces they represent, will determine the nation's prosperity into the next century.

Economic Diversity

Perhaps the most striking aspect of the Swiss economy is its diversity. The country's firms have strong international positions in an amazing range of industries for such a small nation. This range compares favourably with much larger nations and is far wider than that of other small OECD nations like Sweden, Denmark or Austria. It includes food products, chemicals, precision mechanics and optics, process machinery, heavy engineering, electronics and electrical equipment. The breadth and depth of Switzerland's service sector is particularly noteworthy. Financial services (banking and insurance), commercial and logistical services (trading and freight forwarding), business services (management consulting, human resources services and temporary help), medical services, education and tourism are areas of particular strength. The international position of the Swiss service sector is matched only by that of the United States and of the biggest European countries. Expertise in service industries also contributes to the success of many other industries throughout the economy.

Chemicals: Switzerland's strength in the chemical industry belies the nation's small size. Switzerland accounts for roughly one per cent of world output in the chemical industry. Chemical exports exceeded Sfr. 17.8 billion, or more than 21 per cent of total exports, in 1989. These figures drastically understate the positions of the leading chemical firms in Switzerland, Basle-based Ciba-Geigy, Sandoz and Hoffmann-La Roche, each of which has extensive overseas operations. Swiss firms have particularly strong positions in pharmaceuticals, flavours and fragrances and dyestuffs with world market shares of 10 per cent, 12 per cent and 20 per cent respectively.

Textiles and Apparel: The textile and apparel industry has been of great significance to the development of the Swiss economy. Switzerland was the world's leading supplier of cotton yarn and fabric in the 18th century. Zurich was Europe's second leading silk centre after Lyon, while Basle was the leading centre of the ribbon industry. The textile industry helped spawn Switzerland's machinery, chemical, banking and trading industries. The textile industry itself began a long decline in the early 19th century with the advent of industrialisation in England and the rise of trade barriers. Total exports in the textile and apparel sector were nearly Sfr. 5 billion in 1989. Even though the sector ran a trade deficit of Sfr. 3.5 billion overall, Swiss firms continued to be leading suppliers of fine cotton, embroidery, silk and satin for the high-fashion apparel industry.

Machinery Industries: Swiss firms compete in a wide range of machinery industries. Machinery exports exceeded Sfr. 19 billion, or 22.5 per cent of total exports in 1989. Switzerland is the world's third leading exporter of textile machinery, the third leading exporter of machine tools, and the third leading exporter of graphic machines. Other areas of strength include machinery for grain milling, printing, paper processing and plastics processing. Many of the nation's machinery industries export more than 90 per cent of their output each year.

In textile machinery, Switzerland is home to the world leaders in looms (Sulzer), dobbies (Stäubli), embroidery machinery (Saurer) and narrow fabric weaving machines (Jacob Mueller), as well as the world's second leading producer of spinning machines (Rieter). Most of the nation's 100 machine tool companies are small or medium-sized firms. Many are leaders in particular market niches, such as Maegerle in electrostatic grinding machines. Other machinery firms with worldwide reputations include Bobst in cardboard packaging equipment, SIG in chocolate processing and packaging equipment, and Bühler in grain milling machines.

Heavy engineering has been another Swiss specialty. Switzerland is the world's leading producer of marine diesel engines, despite the fact that it has no sea coast. Schindler is the world's second leading elevator and escalator company. SIG, SLM, ABB and Alusuisse are active in railway and subway equipment. ABB received more than Sfr. 1 billion in orders for city rail and subway systems in 1989 alone. SLM accounts for some 70 per cent of the world's rack railways, while von Roll is the world leader in funiculars, gondola cable ways and ski lifts. (1)

Watch Industry: Swiss firms account for approximately 50 per cent of the world watch market by value and 15 per cent by unit volume. Exports reached a record Sfr. 6 billion in 1989. Switzerland is the home of the world's two leading watch producers, SMH and Rolex. While the Swiss position in low and medium-priced watches has come under attack, first from American firms and then from Japanese and Asian firms, luxury watch firms such as Rolex, Ebel, Vacheron & Constantin, Audemars Piguet, Patek Philippe, Piaget and Blancpain have not been seriously challenged in more than 200 years. Today they account for more than 85 per cent of worldwide sales of luxury watches.

Precision Mechanics and Optics: Swiss firms have a long tradition in the precision mechanical and optical industries. In 1989, exports in these categories reached Sfr. 4.3 billion. Mettler, long the world leader in precision balances and scales, recently acquired Toledo (U.S.) and became the world's largest supplier. In the optical sector, Leica is among the world leaders in surveying equipment, precision optical measuring devices and lenses for satellite photography.

Electrical and Electronics Industries: Swiss firms are increasingly important in electrical and electronic products. Staefa Control, Landis & Gyr and Sauter are among Europe's leading suppliers of heating, ventilation and air conditioning (HVAC) controls. Other well-known firms include Cerberus in fire detection equipment, Huni in process controls for the tanning industry, Zellweger Uster in controls for textile machinery and Sprecher & Schuh in low voltage electrical switchgear. Medical electronics firms are also on the rise. Phonak, Rexton and Gfeller are major hearing aid manufacturers and Sulzer, after its acquisition of the American firm Intermedics, is a leading supplier of pacemakers.

Financial Services: Switzerland has been a centre for financial services since the 16th century. The larger banks got their start in the middle of the 19th century when financing the national railroad proved beyond the capabilities of existing institutions. In the following decades, high economic growth, savings that exceeded domestic needs, low inflation, external surpluses, sound government financial policies, political neutrality, bank secrecy and a universal banking system all stimulated the growth of the financial service sector. Banking is presently Switzerland's largest single foreign exchange earner, accounting for more than Sfr. 16 billion in net surplus in 1989.

Particularly strong sectors include portfolio management, international underwriting and precious metal trading. The big banks, Union Bank, Credit Suisse and Swiss Bank Corporation, are among the world's largest institutional investors and underwriters. Switzerland is by far the world's leader in offshore placed funds, with particular strength in managing funds for wealthy individuals. Zurich, the world's leading centre for precious metal trading, accounts for some 40 to 50 per cent of world gold trade.

Tourism: Switzerland is a favourite destination for approximately Sfr. 9.2 billion in 1989, or approximately 3.9 per cent of GDP. International travel payments added another Sfr. 2.3 billion to Swiss coffers. The country has more than 6,700 hotels and is the home of the legendary alpine resorts of St. Moritz, Gstaad, Zermatt and Davos. Cities like Lucerne and Montreux are major tourist destinations. Tens of thousands also flock each year to Switzerland's numerous spas, or take part in short courses that are a mix of education and tourism.

Commercial Services: Many firms have been internationally successful in a range of commercial and logistical services. Trading companies, such as André, UTC, UHAG, Siber Hegner, Desco von Schulthess and Volkart, carry on a centuries-old merchant tradition. Many began as traders between Europe and Asian or African markets more than a century ago. Three of the world's leading freight forwarding firms are Swiss (Danzas, Kühne & Nagel and Panalpina). The two firms, Société Générale de Surveillance (SGS), by far the world leader, and Inspectorate International, provide inspection, trade monitoring and customs services on a worldwide basis. Adia is the world's second leading supplier of temporary help. Swiss firms have an important position in the rapidly growing environmental engineering sector, with exports of Sfr. 2 billion in 1989.

A Philosophy of Quality

Swiss firms almost invariably compete in the most sophisticated segments in their industries. This is true in chocolate, chemicals, machinery, watches, optics, textiles and consumer goods. Swiss firms developed the premium chocolate market and have become the yardstick by which all others are measured. The chemical industry is far more concentrated in high value segments than that of any other country. Some of the world's finest cottons, silks, satins and embroidery come from Switzerland. Swiss firms specialise in the most advanced segments of the textile machinery, machine tools and packaging machinery industries, where they compete with top quality, precise and reliable equipment. Switzerland has no auto industry, but a Swiss firm, Sauber, designs and builds championship racing cars for Mercedes-Benz. Phonak is the world leader in high-gain hearing aids for those with severe hearing loss.

Swiss firms are obsessed with quality. As one executive put it, 'Quality is our business.' In many cases, quality is both a strategy and a philosophy. Quality is a way of competing, a source of pride, and a spur to improvement and innovation. This philosophy of quality can be seen in the art and craftsmanship of an Audemars Piguet mechanical watch or the precision construction of a Leica theodolite, heard in the sound of a Studer Revox tape machine or a Phonak hearing aid, or tasted in Lindt and Sprüngli chocolate or a fine Gruyère cheese. Hotels and banks are known for their high quality services. Swissair, the national airline, typically ranks as number one or two among major airlines in surveys of on-time performance and customer satisfaction. In industry after industry, 'Swiss made' is a hallmark of quality known throughout the world. Swiss managers and workers take naturally to this emphasis on quality. They become personally involved in the process and take personal responsibility for the outcome. While some firms explicitly manage for quality, others rely on the personal and professional desire for quality on the part of their managers and workers.

A Tradition of Innovation

Innovation has been at the core of Switzerland's economic success. Nestlé and its forerunners were the first to introduce baby foods (1867), milk chocolate (1875), dehydrated soups (1886) and instant coffee (1938). The chemical industry has been a hotbed of innovation for more than a century. Ciba-Geigy and Sandoz became leaders in dye technology in the latter portion of the 19th century. Major breakthroughs were made in pesticides at Geigy in the '30s, and synthetic hormones and vitamins at Ciba and La Roche, respectively, in the '40s. Librium and Valium, developed by La Roche in the early '60s, proved to be two of the best-selling drugs in history. These firms and their scientists have maintained their focus on innovation. A recent study of pharmaceutical innovation placed them second only to American firms in the introduction of new drugs from 1975 to 1986.

The Swiss have made numerous innovations in products, processes and marketing in the watch industry. They were the first to use precision machine–tools and interchangeable parts for watches and the first to produce affordable wrist watches for mass markets. The Swatch represented a major marketing innovation, which turned the inexpensive watch into a fashion item, as well as a major process innovation. The unique styling of Tissot and Rado watches has done the same for medium-priced watches. Virtually all the advances in the design and production of luxury watches in the last two centuries have been made by Swiss.

The Swiss have also been innovative in machinery and electronics. Rudolphe Lindt developed the modern chocolate-refining process and the appropriate equipment in the latter portion of the 19th century. Brown and Boveri made several innovations in electrical generation and transmission equipment. The Sulzer brothers were instrumental in the development of the diesel engine in the 1880s and 1890s. Sulzer introduced the projectile loom in 1950 and has virtually monopolised the segment ever since. A series of innovations by founder Walter Reist has made Ferag the world leader in post production equipment for the newspaper industry. Füllemann Engineering has achieved success with a new burner design that minimises the pollution from burning home heating oil. Several recent innovations by Komax engineers have made the company the world leader in wire processing machinery.

Cerberus developed the ionisation smoke detector, invented by a physics student at the Federal Institute of Technology (ETH) in the '40s, and now provides a whole range of fire detection systems. Staefa Control based its first building control equipment on a new magnetic valve for heating and ventilation controls invented by a Swiss ventilation engineer in the '60s. The computer mouse was developed by a team from Logitech, which has also achieved success with its 'Scan-Man' scanners and associated software.

Pressure, Investment and Openness in the Swiss Economy

The ability to compete on quality and innovation has been developed through pressure, investment and openness to outside influences. Pressures have forced Swiss firms to compete on quality and innovation; investments have provided them with the requisite capabilities; openness has been a source of new ideas and talented individuals. The presence of different cultures within the nation has also proved to be an advantage, the Swiss deal fluidly with foreign customers, suppliers and employees. Swiss firms and individuals have also been extremely pragmatic and flexible in their outlook.

Pressure: The Swiss economy has been formed by pressure and challenge. Switzerland was a relatively poor country for centuries. People, both emigrants and mercenaries, were a major export. Limited resources and difficult farming conditions forced Swiss people to take up manufacturing and trading at an early date. The watch industry in the Jura and the textile industry in Eastern Switzerland provided much needed employment in areas with limited agricultural potential. Engineering, surveying equipment and transportation equipment firms sprang up in the 19th century as Switzerland attempted to build a transportation infrastructure in a tough, mountainous environment. The big banks developed around the same time, in part to finance the infrastructure investments.

The nature of domestic demand has challenged firms to continually improve and upgrade their products and processes. Swiss industrial customers, who are often world leaders in their own industries, demand the highest quality inputs and machinery. The textile machinery industry, for example, sells only 5 per cent of its output in Switzerland.

Even so, Swiss customers are among the world's most demanding buyers of textile machinery, since in order to be competitive with a high wage structure, they must produce the highest quality products and use the highest quality equipment.

Tough environmental regulations have been instrumental to the growth of the Swiss environmental engineering industry.

The Swiss are among the world's most demanding buyers of consumer products. High incomes allow consumers to shop for quality, while expectations of perfection make them particularly difficult to please. Consumer-products companies, such as Nestlé, Bally, Victorinox, the watch companies and others, have been able to capitalise on the skills they have developed in satisfying demanding local consumers. High wages, high infrastructure costs and an appreciating currency have forced Swiss firms to move into ever higher productivity segments and industries. They must continually innovate to supply new and improved products. Swiss multinationals focus the highest value activities in Switzerland and move more routine activities to foreign subsidiaries. This process forces them to continually develop new, higher productivity activities.

Investment: The most important investments a nation can make are in its people. High levels of public and private investment characterise education and training. The excellence of the schools and universities reflects the high value placed on education within the nation. The Federal Institute of Technology in Zurich (ETH) has been particularly noteworthy as a source of new ideas and technically trained people since the middle of the 19th century. The pharmaceutical, chemical, optical, electronics and engineering industries have all profited from their contacts with the ETH. The Federal Institute of Technology in Lausanne (EPFL) has close relations with a large number of domestic and foreign firms. One such relationship, with Thomson of France, has resulted in advances in electronic imaging, lasers and high frequency transistors. The University at St. Gall is widely regarded as one of the best undergraduate business schools in Europe, while IMD is one of Europe's leading graduate schools of business.

Approximately 25 per cent of Swiss teenagers go on to college. Another 70 per cent go through three or four year apprenticeship programmes that combine schooling with on-the-job training. Apprenticeship programmes provide education, job training and youth employment, major problem areas in many nations. Apprenticeship programmes and their graduates are highly respected, and rightly so. Many of the nation's corporate and political leaders have been through apprenticeship programmes. In many other nations, including most of the English speaking world, apprenticeship and vocational training programmes are viewed as distinctly second class, and therefore do not get support. The result is that instead of 'workers,' the Swiss system turns out skilled technicians, craftsmen and professionals.

Swiss firms also invest heavily in training programmes for employees and management. SGS, for example, puts new employees through a nine-month training programmes. The three large banks each spend in excess of Sfr. 45 million a year on their own formal management training programmes. ABB invests over Sfr. 40 million a year on training efforts that include a 1,000 person apprentice programme, its own technical school and a series of management training programmes.

As a nation, Switzerland invests aggressively in research and development. Only Sweden invests a larger portion of GDP in R&D. R&D employees account for a higher percentage of total employment in Switzerland than in any other OECD nation. As a result, more patents are issued each year to Swiss residents, on a per capita basis, than to residents of any other country. The private sector provides nearly 80 per cent of the nation's R&D funding, the highest percentage among OECD nations. Large and small Swiss firms are committed to R&D. Small firms, in fact, spend a higher proportion of their sales on R&D than their large counterparts. Several Swiss firms fund additional research beyond that for their own products and processes. The Nestlé Research Centre, with an annual budget of over Sfr. 100 million, is the world's largest centre devoted to food and nutrition research. The Centre has a diverse portfolio of research programmes, including research on basic nutrition and food allergies. The chemical companies fund independent research institutes such as the Roche Institute for Molecular Biology in the United States (La Roche), the Institute for Immunology in Basle (La Roche), and the Friedrich Miescheler Institute in Basle (Ciba-Geigy) in addition to their own substantial in-house R&D efforts. The fertile Swiss research environment has also attracted R&D centres of several foreign firms, such as IBM, as well as international scientific centres, such as CERN.

The time horizon of an investment is often as important as its magnitude. The Swiss tend to invest for the long haul. Relatively few of their firms have the short-term view so prevalent in the United States. The development of the Sulzer loom took nearly 20 years. The Jungfrau railroad, designed for the tourist trade, took some 16 years to complete (1896 to 1912) and is still regarded as a marvel of engineering achievement. The international networks of the leading Swiss multinationals required decades of investment to develop.

Openness to Foreign Influences: Swiss firms have been open to foreign influences and internationalisation. Immigrants have been influential in several important industries. French Huguenots were instrumental in the development of the watch and textile industries. French and German chemists figured prominently in the early days of the chemical industry. Both of the founders of Brown (British) Boveri (German) were foreigners. A German, Diesel, was responsible for Sulzer's entrance into diesel engines. The Anglo-Swiss Condensed Milk Company, one of the principal forerunners of the modern day Nestlé, was founded by two brothers from Illinois. The development of several resorts, including St. Moritz, was heavily influenced by foreigners, who also invented many of the winter sports that make the resorts so popular. Swiss firms are among the most international of all companies. The largest register more than 95 per cent of their sales outside of the home country. Several are far-flung multinationals that were forced to look abroad at an early date due to the small size of the domestic market. They were quick to seize opportunities abroad in foods, chemicals, machinery and financial services. The Swiss commercial service firms are truly global in character. Most of the goods handled by the trading and freight forwarding firms never touch home territory. Only a small fraction of the inspection companies' business is in Switzerland. Swiss firms have been able to leverage their expertise, trustworthiness and the quality of the goods and services they provide worldwide.

A Mixture of Cultures: Swiss firms have taken advantage of the cultural diversity within their own country and of cultural similarities with surrounding nations. Switzerland's German-, French- and Italian-speaking areas make the nation an ideal test market for European sales. Similarities between the domestic and German educational systems, product standards and economies have allowed for a high degree of interaction between domestic and German firms. Swiss optical firms employ a number of people who received their training in Germany. Ferag has worked closely with German newspapers to develop new products. The chemical industry has benefited from technical tie-ups and supply relationships with the leading German chemical firms.

The flavours and fragrances industry provides an excellent example of the successful mix of cultures found in Switzerland: Givaudan was founded in 1895 by two brothers originally from Lyon, France. One brother studied chemistry at the Federal Institute of Technology in Zurich while the other ran the family business in France. Eventually, the brothers set up a company in Geneva, roughly halfway between Lyon and Zurich. Here the combination of French perfume tradition and German-style chemical training resulted in one of the world's leading flavours and fragrances firms. Geneva soon became the centre of the flavour and fragrance industry. To this day, the combination of technical skills and 'nose' of the Geneva perfumers remains unmatched.

Pragmatism and Flexibility: The Swiss tend to be pragmatic, rather than theoretical. In the economic arena, as one Swiss professor wrote nearly thirty years ago, 'The Swiss have much business sense but do not care much to think about economics. This is perhaps one of the reasons why [the] Swiss economy is running so smoothly.'(2) The Swiss also have a very pragmatic attitude toward innovation. They do not innovate simply to innovate, rather they innovate in order to create new or improved products for the marketplace. Similarly, they focus on quality as a means to an end, as a way to satisfy customer needs.

This often involves extensive after-sales service and training of customer personnel to ensure that the maximum value is provided. Finally, Swiss firms and individuals have shown a remarkable ability to adapt products, processes and management to new conditions in foreign nations.

Cause for Concern

Switzerland's economic success is indisputable, but if one looks beneath the surface of the nation's prosperity, there is cause for concern. Productivity growth has been relatively sluggish over the last two decades. Firms face high wages and high costs for inputs and infrastructure. While the first side of the Swiss economy is flexible and pragmatic, there is another side that is far less pragmatic and flexible. This side looks inward rather than outward, resists rather than welcomes change, and is governed by political rather than market forces. It is this side that has caused some Swiss to believe the system that has proven so successful may not be adequate to deal with the challenges of the future.

Uncompetitive Sectors: There are several sectors of the economy in which performance has been less than admirable. The agricultural sector is a prime example. Subsidies and higher prices due to protection account for roughly 80 per cent of farm revenue. Self-sufficiency and support for tourism are frequently given as reasons for Swiss agricultural policy. The reality has more to do with the political organisation of local farmers and the difficulty of organising consumers. Whatever the reason, Swiss consumers pay five to ten times as much for certain foods than the residents of neighbouring countries. It is estimated that Swiss agricultural policy costs the nation in the order of Sfr. 7 billion a year in subsidies and higher prices. Some think the figure is understated.

The domestic portion of the Swiss economy is rife with cartels and monopolies, in distribution, construction, printing, publishing and government contracting, that are inefficient and drain resources from the economy. Despite recent efforts by the Federal Cartel Commission in the insurance and banking sectors, thousands of agreements that limit competition remain. These reduce incentives to upgrade firm capabilities and result in high prices for consumers. Limited competition in automobile importing, for example, results in Swiss consumers paying from 10 per cent to in excess of 60 per cent more for a new car than consumers in neighbouring countries.

Monopolies in Swiss infrastructure are becoming increasingly expensive. The PTT, which has been relatively slow to modernise, could prove costly to industry as information and communication become more important to a nation's competitiveness. Local telecommunication equipment companies, with a protected local market, have never become internationally competitive. Government procurement has often been used to protect Swiss firms, a practice that often results in inefficiency.

Corporate Governance: The Swiss corporate governance system allows companies to resist change. According to the Swiss corporation law, firms can restrict information flows, share ownership and voting rights. Minimal reporting requirements, unreported reserves and restrictions on share ownership and voting rights may enable management to take a long-term view and ensure that Swiss firms are not purchased by foreigners. They can also reduce the capital market's ability to force change and can entrench incompetent management. As a result, shares in Swiss companies are worth far less than they might be. Some firms have a stock market value that is only one fourth or one fifth that of comparable American firms. Attempts to revise the corporation law have met with little success for the past 20 years, despite increasing pressure from institutional investors and foreign governments for changes in governance structures and shareholder rules.

Competitive Difficulties: Many of Switzerland's major manufacturing concerns have come under increasing pressure over the last two decades. Employment in the watch industry halved in the '70s and halved again in the '80s. Major manufacturing companies, such as Sulzer, Brown Boveri, Saurer, von Roll, Georg Fischer and Oerlikon-Bührle saw profitability dwindle. Sulzer sold a majority stake in its marine diesel operations in 1990 and became a takeover target. Saurer exited the truck industry after substantial losses and was eventually taken over. Brown Boveri merged with the Swedish firm, ASEA, after several years of lack-lustre performance. The optical company Kern was taken over by Wild (later renamed Leica) after falling on hard times. In most instances, foreign competition had increased, while in some, uninspired management and resistance to change appear to have been contributing factors.

Failure to Adopt Innovations: There are some signs that Swiss companies may be slower to adopt innovations than they were in the past. The quartz watch movement was first developed in Switzerland, but the domestic watch industry was far slower to adopt it than Japanese and American firms. Leica developed the world's first autofocus camera. Japanese firms, however, were the first to commercially exploit the new technology. The Swiss financial sector has been relatively slow to adopt innovations in securities. Swiss companies, universities and polytechnics failed to keep up with the electronics and computer revolution of the early '80s. In fact, several Swiss firms have had to obtain electronics, computer and software expertise from American partners or subsidiaries. There has been increasing concern about the lack of competitiveness in some of the technologies of the future. In the '60s, high technology goods comprised a far greater portion of Swiss exports than those of any other nation. By 1990, Switzerland's relative position had deteriorated dramatically. Given the importance of competing on innovation in the Swiss context, this is a troubling trend.

Cumbersome Political Process: The Swiss political process is complex and cumbersome. No political party has had a majority since 1919, so Swiss Governments are coalitions that require a great deal of compromise. Widespread consultation and compromise can result in a slow process and less than optimal legislation. Swiss-style direct democracy also allows for government by referendum. The system was designed to make it difficult for the majority to impose its will on the minority. In recent years, the system has been increasingly used by well-organised minority interests to block action by the majority. Ironically, the very flexibility of the political process has, on occasion, made for a paralysed and inflexible policy regime.

In June 1991, a tax reform proposal that would have introduced a value-added tax was defeated in a referendum, despite the fact that it was supported by all four leading political parties, business, and the trade unions. The tax reform was seen as necessary by the business community and as a step towards harmonisation with the EC by the public at large. The reform was defeated even though opinion polls show that the majority in Switzerland favour increasingly close contact and harmonisation with the EC.

Swiss energy policy has reached an impasse. In a 1990 referendum, voters approved a moratorium on construction of new nuclear power plants until at least the year 2000. To fill the void, a 25-year supply agreement was reached with France, which ironically produces nearly all its power in nuclear plants. A proposal to abandon Switzerland's existing nuclear facilities, which supply nearly 40 per cent of the nation's power, 'as quickly as possible' was defeated by voters, but is sure to resurface. Switzerland's energy future remains uncertain, especially since environmental concerns also limit the country's ability to expand hydropower resources, which currently account for 60 per cent of Swiss generating capacity, or to construct fossil fuel-burning facilities.

Business-Government Relations: The relations between business and government within Switzerland are becoming more complex. Business is subject to a bewildering, and sometimes conflicting, array of federal, cantonal and local regulations. These include restrictions on construction, environmental regulation and, in some cases, price controls. Specialty firms have even emerged to guide companies through the complexities. Regulation of business is increasing in Switzerland at a time when deregulation has been the trend around the world.

Relations between the Swiss Government and the banking industry may not be as peaceful as they once were. Swiss bankers were recently dismayed by attempts to place interest rates on mortgages under the authority of the Price Control Board. The Finance Minister has been criticised by members of the financial community for his support of taxes on financial transactions and for failing to modernise financial laws to increase the competitiveness of Swiss firms. He has been quoted as saying that the financial sector has reached its 'permissible limits' and is 'too strong', something anyone familiar with the difficulties faced by the U.S. financial sector would find hard to believe.

Labour Shortages: Switzerland has had a chronic shortage of skilled labour. The chemical, machinery and service sectors have all felt the effects of the shortages. Many firms are choosing to expand abroad rather than in Switzerland. In the past, the foreign subsidiaries of Swiss firms were mostly production or marketing oriented, but now even research and some administrative activities are being moved outside of Switzerland. Science and engineering graduates are in particularly short supply, as are multilingual support personnel.

The concern for the long term is that Switzerland may lose some of the skills that has made its firms successful. Restrictions on immigration have made it very difficult for domestic firms to 'import' needed expertise. There is a danger that these firms will become less open to foreign ideas and that the Swiss environment will become less dynamic and innovative due to a lack of diversity.

Switzerland's External Challenges

A number of external challenges have recently heightened concerns about the economy. The three most important are increasing competition and pressure to reform from other nations, the increasing economic integration of the European Community and the tremendous changes underway in Eastern Europe.

Foreign Competition and Pressure: The level of international competition has risen dramatically over the last two decades. Foreign competitors are major threats for Swiss firms in several important industries. The watch industry came under attack from Japanese and Hong Kong-based firms in the mid-'70s and did not fully adjust until some ten years later. German firms continue to be major competitors in chemicals, optics and machinery industries. Japanese firms have made significant inroads in optics and machinery. Italian firms are becoming more important in a range of machinery industries. As firms from these nations improve the quality of their offerings, Swiss firms must continually improve just to hold their positions.

Switzerland has come under pressure to open closed sectors of the economy. Foreign governments have complained that Switzerland allows its firms to restrict foreign ownership, while they can easily purchase foreign companies. It will be difficult for Switzerland to continue to negotiate open access for manufactured products under the GATT while subsidising its own agriculture and engaging in de facto protection under its public procurement policies. Other countries are increasingly demanding reciprocity, a reciprocity that many in Switzerland may find uncomfortable.

The EC: The EC is Switzerland's leading trading partner, accounting for some 71 per cent of Switzerland's imports and 56 per cent of its exports in 1988. Switzerland is the second leading market for EC exports after the United States and has negotiated more than 120 bilateral agreements with the EC to ensure mutual market access.

The EC's Europe 1992 Programme has raised fears that Swiss firms will be discriminated against in the EC market. In addition, there are fears that EC firms will benefit from research and educational programmes from which Swiss firms and individuals are excluded. As other EFTA members, such as Austria, Sweden, Norway and Finland, seek or contemplate EC membership, there is an increasing chance that Switzerland will be left behind. The present situation has created a level of interest within Switzerland in actually joining the EC that would have been virtually unthinkable only five years ago, when voters rejected membership in the United Nations by a large margin.

There are several internal issues and complicated trade-offs that Switzerland would have to resolve in order to join the EC. The Swiss Constitution guarantees federalism and direct democracy. It will prove difficult for the Swiss to give the EC Commission powers they have not given to their own Federal Government. Swiss agricultural policy would also have to be revised were Switzerland to join the EC. Lowering agricultural supports to EC levels would cause uproar from the farming community. There have already been calls for Switzerland to loosen its restrictive immigration policies for people from EC countries. This would be politically difficult in a nation, where foreigners already account for more than 25 per cent of the workforce, a much higher percentage than any EC nation.

Eastern Europe: The opening of Eastern Europe to the West will provide Switzerland with opportunities and challenges. Swiss capital, equipment and infrastructure-related companies will be in good position to help in the modernisation of Eastern European industry and infrastructure. It is not clear, however, that Eastern European countries are ready for, or can pay for, high quality Swiss products. Exports to Eastern Europe were only Sfr. 2.7 billion in 1989.

The opening of Eastern Europe could have some perverse effects on Switzerland as well. Switzerland has taken advantage of its position as a neutral country at the centre of Europe. The value of this neutrality may be diminished as Eastern European countries become more Western in outlook. In addition, tensions in Eastern Europe may create a wave of refugees. Other Western European nations are likely to pressure Switzerland to do its part in taking in a portion of these refugees.

Switzerland's Economic Future

What does the future hold for the Swiss economy? In the past, the pragmatic, open and dynamic side of the economy has generated the wealth necessary to support the economy's less dynamic side. Unless there is change, this will become an increasing burden in a new competitive environment. Ironically, the external challenges have provided a unique opportunity for the Swiss to reassess the basics of their system, but the greatest challenges that face the economy are not external. The greatest challenge facing the Swiss economy is not the emergence of a unified European market. Swiss firms are integrated into the European economy to a far greater extent than those of several EC members. Many are poised to take advantage of greater unification of the European market from locations within Switzerland or within the EC. Swiss products are highly regarded and tend to fill needs that firms in other countries cannot meet. The same is true of Swiss service firms. The Swiss banking sector, for example, with its reputation for security and quality service, is extremely well positioned to take advantage of the free flow of funds expected within Europe.

Calls for Switzerland to join the EC are therefore premature. It will take some time for the EC to digest the 1992 Programme. Switzerland can probably negotiate mutual access as it has done in the past. It is not at all clear that the country's interests would be better served by becoming one of 13 or 18 members of an expanded EC. In any event, the question is moot for the time being, the EC is not accepting applications for membership until 1993. The greatest challenge for the Swiss economy is not the opening of Eastern Europe to the West. Opportunities will certainly exist, but it will be some time before Eastern European companies and consumers will fully appreciate, or be able to afford, large quantities of Swiss products. Until then, the greatest opportunities will be in infrastructure, engineering and consulting of all types.

Even with a lessening of tensions between East and West, the value of Switzerland's neutrality and central position will not be greatly diminished. There will always be a need for the nations of the world to find a neutral ground where they can meet to discuss their differences. As the frequency of East-West contact increases, Switzerland's geographic position may become even more important than before.

The Challenge of Prosperity: The greatest challenge to Swiss prosperity is prosperity itself. The greatest danger faced by the Swiss economy is complacency. There is a growing tendency to look inward for safety and comfort, rather than outward for challenge and pressure. Several observers have remarked that it is becoming more difficult to get Swiss people to accept overseas postings. There are signs of an increasing focus on redistributing existing wealth rather than creating new wealth. Students are increasingly favouring law and accountancy to engineering and sciences. Government spending, though still low by international standards, is growing rapidly. Competition is not as valued as it once was. The desire to preserve and protect is quite natural, but is counter-productive in the long run. The Swiss economy has been the best example of the truism that it is pressure, investment and innovation that lead to economic success in the modern world, that the skills and capabilities of a nation's people are far more important than inherited resources. Switzerland must not turn inward, or seek to reduce pressures. Instead, it should address the new competitive realities as it has in the past, by investing in innovation and in people, and by being open and pragmatic.

It will be difficult for the political process, which by necessity has to focus on local and even parochial issues, to be the major agent of change. Given the decentralised nature of the Swiss system, this is not as alarming as it might be. Economic change within Switzerland rarely comes from Berne, the centre of the Federal Government. Instead, it comes from forward looking companies and individuals. These must impress on others the need for change at the national level in areas such as tax reform, immigration policy and rationalisation of the regulatory environment.

Swiss managers and workers seem ready to make changes to address these new competitive realities. They understand that their firms must continue to innovate and upgrade their capabilities. To quote La Roche's Andreas Leuenberger, 'Today's success is far from being a guarantee for success in the future. In a world of change, there is no justification for sitting back and feeling content.'(3). Managers have told me that operating in Switzerland has never been easy, but that the current situation has increased the pressures within the economy. At the same time, many managers and labor leaders are becoming more vocal critics of the inefficiencies and difficulties of operating within Switzerland.

Switzerland will continue to be one of the world's richest nations, but adjustments will be necessary to achieve maximal prosperity. There are a number of encouraging signs. The nation has an extraordinary economic base. A number of firms, such as Saurer, Sulzer and ABB, are showing signs of revitalisation. Medical technology, environmental engineering and financial services are areas of increasing opportunity. Swiss companies are beginning to open up their share registries, albeit very slowly. Cartels in the financial services sector are being eliminated, while others are facing increased scrutiny.

The most encouraging sign, however, is that Swiss people are increasingly questioning the status quo. This questioning is necessary to eliminate inefficiencies and to avoid lapsing into a false sense of security. If the Swiss continue to invest, to innovate and to question, the next century will be a bright one for the Swiss economy.

Notes:

This essay draws upon *Michael E. Porter*, The Competitive Advantage of Nations, (New York: The Free Press, 1990); and *Silvio Borner, Michael Porter, Rolf Weder, and Michael Enright*, Internationale Wettbewerbsvorteile: Ein strategisches Konzept für die Schweiz, (Frankfurt: Verlag NZZ, 1991).

1. 'Riding High,' Swiss Business, January/February 1990, pp.52-53.
2. *Arnold C. Hunold*, The Industrial Development of Switzerland, (Cairo: The National Bank of Egypt, 1954), p.1
3. Quoted in 'Management by Medicine Man,' Swiss Business, January/February 1991, p.6.

Swiss Banks as a Discreet Culture
Shuhei Hosokawa

The Myth of the Swiss Banks

The myth of the Swiss banks is as widespread as it is notorious. In no way does it correspond to the truth, and yet it is deeply rooted in people's imaginations throughout the world. No other nation is so closely associated with banking. Switzerland's role in the banking world is similar to that played by the Vatican in the world of Catholicism. In both cases, deep secrets are concealed behind gleaming façades. Not only foreigners but the Swiss, too, see the banks as a typical expression of their self-image.

The composer Rolf Liebermann, who was born in Zurich in 1910, wrote the piece '3x1=CH+X' for Switzerland's 700-year anniversary celebrations. It was premiered at Zurich Opera House in September 1991. '3x1' refers to the alliance of the three original Swiss cantons. 'CH' represents Swiss tolerance for the cultural and linguistic minorities in the country. 'X' refers to the unknown quantity of 'Europe'. The plus sign indicates that Switzerland as a state may be on the periphery of Europe, but that integration is probably indispensable, if not indeed, inevitable. The right-hand side of this remarkable equation thus symbolises the present and the future of Switzerland. The equals sign embodies the cultural identity that Switzerland has preserved for 700 years. The piece is not intended to encapsulate or conceal the country's 700-year history, but rather celebrates the fact that Switzerland can be held up as a model in the modern world.

Post-war composers often devote great care to the titling of their works but such a direct reference to the composer's own country is rare. At a press conference before the première, Liebermann even referred to the banks: 'We're doing far too little for our reputation abroad. Small wonder that someone like Jean Ziegler, whose writing is often critical of the banks, shapes the image of Switzerland in France, and small wonder, too, that the Germans write about our banks in exclusively negative terms. We must draw more attention to our ethical and cultural values.'

Every country has its economic corruption and financial scandals, including Japan. But there not even the most moral of artists could conceive of composing a work to restore a lost faith in international finance. Trust in the banks is apparently just as vital and significant as trust in the people: cautious and careful service on the part of the banks corresponds to cautious and careful concern for the people. Illegal actions by banks are a national crime. In Switzerland the banks are not only organisations that manage finances, but institutions that define our 'ethical and cultural values' - they have their own culture and their own ethics. It is precisely this that lends an almost mythical aura to the Swiss banks. Neither the style and quality of their activities, nor their long and complicated history, exert a particular psychological force on the Swiss; instead, somewhat like the independent William Tell and the sublime Alps, they have become enveloped in a wealth of connotations. It would be impossible to write a history of the origins of the national awareness in Switzerland without including the banks in the picture.

Swiss Banks in a State of Flux

Swiss banks are in a state of flux. I heard these words over and over again whenever I met Swiss bankers. Just as Switzerland does not only have banks, neither is Switzerland the only country that has banks. Swiss banks are faced increasingly with a situation of international competition. They have lost ground to the Japanese and American banks on a number of occasions already. There are at least four interrelated causes for this change:

1. the end of the Swiss banking cartel and the transition to free competition,
2. the change in the hierarchy system, which meant the introduction of American principles of management,
3. reform of the education system with the new requirement of a university degree or equivalent qualifications, and
4. the influence of the European Community with its requirement of complete openness in all business dealings.

The building of the Swiss Credit Bank on Zurich's Paradeplatz with its ornate 19th-century facade, is unusually imposing for a Swiss bank. You walk into an entrance hall with marble floors and thick, round Greek columns. In the lift, the buttons for the floors onto which I was not allowed were disconnected, because the porter had already been told that I had arranged an appointment with 31-year-old investment consultant Hans-Jürg Zuber. I was not to wander out onto another floor either by accident or by intention. The lift only stopped on the correct floor. As I walked into Mr Zuber's office I heard the sound of soft rock music. He immediately turned down MTV. I had been told the televisions that I saw in every office during my series of appointments were there to pick up CNN news. Thin tie over a snow-white shirt; well-cut, short blond hair; a boyish face with an intelligent expression; the alert answers – it all corresponded with my idea of a 'competent young banker'. He was the very image of a yuppie. When I asked him if he had seen the Hollywood films *Wall Street* and *Bonfire of the Vanities*, he answered, somewhat piqued: ' I don't like to have bankers confused with brokers or dealers. Bankers are not out for adventure. It is an enormous mistake to imagine that you can immediately drive around in a Porsche and spend the weekend in a villa on the lake the minute you join the banking world.' The yuppie image of certain bankers is based chiefly on the fact that outsiders cannot draw a clear distinction between the wealth of the client and that of his investment consultant. As Zuber sees it, there are 'two kinds of money in a bank: other people's money, which is the substance of my work, and my own much more modest account, which I use for my own happiness. Of course one of the peculiarities of money is that there is never enough, however much of it you have. But that is not to say that happiness is exclusively dependent on it.'

Hans-Jürg Zuber comes from St Moritz; as he told me he pointed to a poster on the white wall showing a turn-of-the-century skier. After graduating from business school he worked in a small bank with only fourteen employees. There he was fortunate enough to experience the drama of a bank from the dressing-room to the stage performance. Mr Zuber points out that this cannot occur within the framework of a three-year apprenticeship in a large bank, because of its high degree of specialisation. In 1990 he visited New York to study what he called the 'American way of banking '. The experience made him painfully aware of the difference between the careful practices of Swiss banks and the financial engineering in the United States. The United States can be seen as a model in this field. If one seeks to transfer the 'American way' in investment banking to prevailing conditions in Switzerland, there appear to be certain deficiencies in the training of a Swiss banker, for instance an economics degee is indispensable in the States. In today's competitive situation, American management strategies, where team spirit and performance occupy centre stage, are increasingly important. Certainly, Switzerland and America do not have the same traditions. The mentality of the private banker, with its emphasis on individual client contact and attentive service, is unrivalled.

Mr Zuber chose his profession, he told me, because he enjoys the personal contact with other people, and with people with money who want to do something especially interesting with it. Zuber is convinced that the task of the investment consultant consists on the one hand of establishing a synthesis between his knowledge and the client's money, and on the other of steering the best possible middle course between risk and high-performance. In no way is investment a 'game'. He does not think that you can justify playing with other people's money. The conventional attitude that 'the client is king' is quite apparent; and his attitude is quite unlike the cold snobbery of the yuppie as depicted in American films. This tradition on the part of Swiss banks informed my whole conversation with Mr Zuber.

A Classicist

Robert Holzach was born in 1922. He comes closest to my idea of the classical banker. Thinning white hair, a grey suit and eyes that can motivate people. There are deep wrinkles between his eyes, testimony perhaps, to a reflective character. He expresses himself in very logical and persuasive language. A VIP in the Swiss banking world; in 1976 he was appointed to the office of the President of the Union Bank of Switzerland, from 1980 that of the President of the Administrative Council and in 1988 the Honorary Chairmanship. If I was the director of a Japanese advertising company I would have used Mr Zuber in advertisements for Californian sparkling wine and Mr Holzach in advertisements for cognac.

After taking a Doctorate in Law from Zurich University (1949), he became a lawyer. He joined UBS as a trainee in 1951 and was to stay with them for a further forty years. His happiest professional experience was when he lent an electrician with a small firm 35,000 Francs, and the electrician then went on to become Switzerland's industry leader. If he had not given him the credit at that point, the electrical company in question would probably be nothing special today. His saddest experience was the great disappointment he felt when he witnessed large-scale errors within the bank. In 1974, foreign exchange speculations by the bank lost a customer 140 million Francs. The worst thing about the event was the abuse of trust within the bank that it represented and the crisis that it provoked.

The opening of the Wolfsberg training centre in 1975, on the other hand, was another moment of great personal happiness because his and the bank's personnel-manager's long-cherished ambition to set up a training institute for bankers was finally fulfilled. The institute provides comprehensive studies in professional management and general education as well as banking. Holzach's opening speech was entitled: 'Can our age do without an élite?' The edited manuscript was later published in the series 'Wolfsberg Essays'. In the speech Holzach advances the thesis that a contemporary élite must not only contribute its ability and knowledge, but also be aware of its responsibilities to itself and society. For this reason he prefers the title 'entrepreneur' to 'manager'. He thinks the latter is merely an expert in management within an administrative apparatus, while the entrepreneur also bears a responsibility for other activities in society. Society's élite must not isolate itself, for it 'can involve genuine and overall responsibility in its judgments and solutions'. But this responsibility demands a sensitivity to and an awareness of different perspectives. Thus, for him, what is required is not short-term, mathematical and quantitative decisions, but long-term, empirical and qualitative decisions: 'Above all, the banker must learn that mathematics is controlled by intuition, and intuition by experience.' Holzach criticises the younger generation for putting its faith in numbers combined with a tendency to act according to short-term perspectives. The computer has given a further impetus to this way of thinking (or even demands this way of thinking), but history only moves 'in long waves'. Holzach says very confidently that 'qualitative' thought, notoriously unfashionable at present, will soon be rehabilitated. 'I like you' – that's the best possible form of trust. However highly developed electronics may become, personal contact is still inevitable, and the ability to make that contact is entirely based on experience.

At the end of our meeting, he gave me a collection of his speeches with the title: 'Challenges', and with his closing sentence he summed up the banker's entrepreneurial attitude. 'The entrepreneur pushes onwards, because he wants progress.' I should add that Robert Holzach held the rank of colonel in the Swiss Army. The lift was already there when he opened the office door and shook my hand. A smartly-dressed porter stood politely holding the door open.

Transit in Ticino

Mr Generali's office, on the top floor of the Banca del Gottardo in Lugano, is blessed with a wonderful view of the distant Alps. The building was erected by the Ticino architect Mario Botta. While splendid postmodern buildings are built throughout the world, Swiss banks, in contrast, are modest, as they always have been. This building, however, is famous. The brick-red and grey stripes catch the eye from a long way off, although the building does not actually clash with the other banks in the Viale Franscini. The singularity of the edifice lies in its geometrical form, symmetrical principles and beautiful use of light. The ground floor of the left wing of this four-part building contains a gallery, which had opened a little exhibition of books of the series Art & Architecture about Alvar Aalto, Futurism, Surrealism, Andy Warhol and others shortly before my visit. The Banca del Gottardo is proud of its collection of contemporary art; a collection which principally supports younger Swiss artists.

After graduating in economics, Generali worked in the banking sector in Zurich and Lugano before becoming a member of the executive council for a number of years. Ticino is a small canton and a person like Generali acts as a link between politics, business and culture. Politics, business and the army are even more closely linked in Ticino than elsewhere in Switzerland. Relationships of this kind could easily turn into an oligarchy. But Mr Generali is more concerned with the possibility that the political compromise reached 30 years ago is threatening to collapse, and not because 'people are in the process of losing their tolerance, but because the development of the media has changed the political methods of the right and the left.' The polarisation of interests is threatening the 'Swiss way' in politics and economics.

Mr Generali stresses that capital is no longer a national matter. A distinction should not be drawn between national and foreign capital, but between 'serious' (long-term prospects, contributions to the local economy) and 'unserious' capital (including drugs). The Banca del Gottardo, by the way, was bought up by the Japanese Sumitomo Bank some years ago, although nothing has changed in its business policy. The rules of the market do not inquire into nationality. Some places, however, do seem endowed with a gift for luring money.

Ticino was traditionally a poor agricultural canton before the influx of capital from the rebuilt Italy began in the '50s and '60s. Lombardy's money travelled northwards. With 52 banks, Lugano is the third largest financial centre in Switzerland after Zurich and Geneva. In Ticino some twelve per cent of the population work in banking (the average is around seven per cent for the whole of Switzerland), and there is one bank till for every 642 inhabitants (as opposed to one per every 1,688 inhabitants in Switzerland as a whole). The Ticino banks became a general topic of conversation in the '70s and '80s, when various scandals attracted a great deal of media attention.

People tend to say, simplistically, that Ticino is an enclave of Italy. In fact, the complex relationship with Italy and a mentality that is open to Germanic ideas have formed its peculiar cultural identity. In Como in Italy, radios and televisions blare from bars and apartments (particularly when there is a football match), and cars and motor-bikes with strange engines make a terrible racket. Only 20 kms north of this in Lugano, you do not hear any background noise at all. The whole city - no, the whole country, is as quiet as a bank entrance hall. Italians can still feel uncomfortable when they hear a foreign language, but the people of Ticino have no fear of foreign languages. Knowledge of foreign languages is a prerequisite of international business deals. Many Italian businesses have branches or subsidiaries in Ticino which often handle negotiations with foreign companies. Politically, Ticino lies in Switzerland, but the canton is economically integrated with Italy. Lugano, with its wonderful lakeside landscape, acts as a fine membrane between the inner and outer Switzerland absorbing the many latent tensions that occur.

Private Banks in Geneva

The history of the Swiss banking begins, apart from a few local money-lenders, in the mid-15th century, when a branch of the Medici Bank was opened in Geneva. With the power relations among their neighbours in a state of constant turmoil, Swiss banks became the financial backbone for industry and for financing the wars that broke out between the other powers.

There are still banks in Geneva which cultivated contact with the so-called anciens régimes, the absolutist governments of Europe, particularly of France, as early as the 18th century. They are, without exception, all private banks.

In the 19th century there were countless such banks, but their numbers have dwindled since World War II as result of mergers. Of the 21 private banks that remain today, half of them are based on the shores of Lake Geneva. The oldest of them, Hentsch & Cie, merged with Darier & Cie in January 1991. Hentsch & Cie was founded in 1796. When Napoleon asked Henry Hentsch for funds for his Italian campaign in 1797, Hentsch refused to lend him any money, because he was afraid of the risk involved, becoming instead the army paymaster. One of the co-owners of the bank today, Bénédict Hentsch, the seventh generation of the family to become a member of the institution, is convinced that he has inherited the same cautious traits today. As in those days, today's clients are upper middle-class families, businessmen, aristocrats and large property-owners.

The bank's main duty is the secure investment of these families' inheritances, so that they can be passed on without depreciation to the following generation. The bank has connections with some families that go back over several generations. This is a bank, then, from the élite, for the élite and by the élite. You will usually discover that it is a private bank that is at the centre of those fantastic stories in which somebody suddenly becomes a millionaire because some unknown relative has left him an unexpected inheritance. Such surprises do occur, but for the most part the activities of the bank are carried out with a quiet discretion. Private banks are not obliged to publish business reports and for that reason are not permitted to publicly advertise for investments. The many specialists deal personally with the accounts of individual clients, unlike in the large merchant banks, where shareholders' accumulated funds must be reinvested in large projects.

Private banks normally deal only with the money of their clients. On the cover of the brochure of the Hentsch Bank, in small but confident lettering is written : 'Hentsch & Cie, person-to-person banking since 1796'. The traditional discretion of Swiss banks also arose from the need, in times past, to protect the private secrets of the upper middle class. The spirit of the motto, 'the client is king', which now also applies to the merchant banks, was presumably handed down from the private banks. According to Mr Hentsch, this attitude is connected with Calvinism and its respect for individual freedom. The establishment of the private banks is also directly related to the Calvinism which permeated the ruling social classes. Consequently the bank of Darier, Hentsch & Cie still feels committed to a rigid and honest ethos, and is run accordingly.

'Just as the lawyer is responsible for legal questions, and the doctor for matters of health, so the private bank is responsible for financial matters. I see myself as something of a doctor where financial matters are concerned. The doctor doesn't need to advertise, and neither do we, because the customers come to us in a similar way. In medical practice, treatment is not generally begun immediately: patients first look for someone whom they can entrust with their medical worries. For us, too, contact with our clients begins with a counselling discussion. Just as some doctors spend their holidays abroad with wealthy citizens and thus also

have time to advise on marital matters, the client's relationship with the private bank is more than a business relationship. It extends to social life, where the private bank will, for example, write letters of recommendation to an excellent boarding school for the admission of clients' children. This means, of course, that the number of clients must be restricted.' If we could describe the money dealt with by the merchant banks as being like cotton, then the money entrusted to the private banks is a pure silk, which can never lose its beauty. There is no denying that such valuable money exists, and attending to it is a demanding, complex and costly affair.

The Bank of Pictet & Cie, founded in 1805, is the largest of the private banks, with 700 employees and branches in London, Tokyo, Hong Kong. The banking hall is like a drawing-room, except that it is empty. Most clients go straight to the first floor, where they meet their fund manager, with whom they plan their international investments and distribute the risk as sensibly as possible. No iron bars protect the safe these days; nowadays it takes only rapid situational analyses carried out by computer and satellite, a field in which the Pictet Bank excels. What is required is not the short-term gambler's luck of the broker; for the client's descendants are to be taken into account in every decision that is made. For 21 years, Charles Pictet has sat behind the desk he inherited from his forefathers - these days a keyboard and screen have been installed next to it - radiating a confidence that all business difficulties can be overcome. 'Unlike the Hentsch family, which moved here from Prussia, we are an old Geneva family.' A child of Geneva - that is the pride of the Pictet family. Like the family trees of other Geneva families, such as the Lombards or the Odiers, the Pictet family goes back 300 years.

Pictet's principle, which is probably that of all the private banks, entails giving its employees the most comfortable and permanent working relationship in a family atmosphere. Individual employees are treated with the same courtesy as the clients, says the firm's first authorised Japanese business representative, Yukie Suzuki: 'This aspect probably brings the bank very close to the Japanese style of business, but the expectations and responsibility of the individual are incomparably greater than they are in Japan. At the same time the bank has a surprisingly profound and far-sighted perspective. As we are small, we move faster. The daily examination of the international situation in finance and politics is undertaken with extreme care. We were among the first banks to take precautions during the Gulf Crisis.'

Only a few Pictet employees have had a banking apprenticeship, most of them are university graduates or banking experts with years of experience in other banks. Mr Pictet sees himself less as the strict father than as an 'uncle', who pays closes attention to his employees, encourages them and cheers them up. As the bank developed from a family business there exists no detailed organisational chart about the relationships between top and bottom ranks. Analysis and advice are provided, even today, by a team of experts. The fund managers – and there are more than 80 of them – meet three to four times a week to hold a long-distance conference with the foreign branches, at which most decisions are reached on a consensual basis. 'Japanese firms hold meetings every morning, too, but we don't do any gymnastics,' he says, with a twinkle in his eye.

Why does Geneva have so many private banks? Herr Pictet explains this by saying that the city historically acted as a 'turntable' between the Italian and French kingdoms on the one hand and the German Empire on the other. Geneva was late (1815) in joining the Confederation. Without industry, like Zurich, and without a Rhine river-trade, like Basle, Geneva turned to service industry. Calvinism encouraged individual freedom and independence. With all its cosmopolitan Protestants, the city became a meeting-place for ideas and people. Zurich also has a major money market but, unlike Geneva, it is based on its industry. Geneva, on the other hand, is an international meeting-point.

If you spend the afternoon in the park on the shore of Lake Geneva, the thought involuntarily springs to mind that beauty is the thrifty Calvinist's only luxury, and the major international banks there must only be façades designed to fool us. For in Geneva, the business of the banks is done in much more secret places, on thick carpets in muted colours.

Gnomes in Grisons

The people of the Canton of Grisons speak Switzerland's fourth national language: Rhaeto-Romansh, as well as a smattering of German and Italian. It takes an hour and a half on the Intercity train from Zurich to reach the cantonal capital, Chur. The vice-manager of the Swiss Bank Corporation (SBC) in Chur, Edwin Lüdi, was born on Lake Zurich. He entered the banking world after completing his secondary-school education. After seven years in St Moritz with the Swiss Volksbank (SVB), he moved to its headquarters in Berne for a year. As the city atmosphere was not to his liking, he returned to the Canton of Grisons, and in 1978 became manager of the branch of the Banca della Svizzera Italiana in St Moritz. Since 1986 he has worked for the Swiss Bank Corporation. He thinks his 'home' is in commercial banking. Every day he sets off on the two-hour journey from St Moritz, where he lives with his wife and five children, to commute to Chur. In St Moritz he is a member of the Rotary Club and the financial manager of the Catholic parish. He also pursues his hobbies of skiing and mountain-climbing.

He has very strong ties to his home in Grisons. Like the rather reticent and laconic mountain-dwellers, he thinks for a long time before speaking - in comparison to the city bankers - and chooses his words carefully.

The most important branch of commerce in the canton is tourism, with a special emphasis on winter sports. Edwin Lüdi deals with local as well as international clients. The former show the influence of the tough climate and the landscape; rather introverted, even critical. On the one hand, per capita income in the region increased as the international clients moved in, on the other hand some new problems arose, such as developments in the property market and the concomitant increase in property prices.

Although Zurich and Berne are more accessible to foreign clients from the point of view of transport and contact, some of them nonetheless turn to Grisons. Perhaps there are investors who want to pursue their business even during their holidays? Advances in telecommunications mean that there is now no difference between having an account in Zurich and one in St Moritz. Money flows on digital currents.

Zurich, internationally famous as the 'city of gnomes', is emblematic of the whole of Switzerland. The interest of the world is focussed on Zurich. But there are other places in Switzerland, such as St Moritz, that are also capable of maintaining an especially high level of discretion. From Grisons, good business can also be done with the neighbouring Principality of Liechtenstein. Edwin Lüdi says his relations with that little country are exceptionally good. Telecommunications has certainly done away with many boundaries, but topographical conditions obviously continue to affect people's lives. As globalisation progresses, the world is becoming more and more standardised, and regional differences are vanishing. Nevertheless, globalisation will never lead to complete standardisation. There will always be a part of the regional character that can not be digitalised; a little 'local knowledge', astutely applied to the inhabitants and their region, will always remain an important criterion of judgement. Financial relationships cannot be maintained only by telephone, fax machine or computer. Like Edwin Lüdi, some of the money also has an affinity with Grisons. Lüdi deals with tourist money, but he is also a travel guide around the world of financial tourism.

The Collector's Corner

It would be hard for anyone to replace him. Certainly, the existence of two or three colleagues means that Meinrad Schnellmann can indulge to the full his hobby of mountaineering without any worries. He is a kind of uncrowned king of the 'alternative stock-exchange', where some 600 non-admitted Swiss shares are traded. Some 100 to 150 transactions are conducted daily. The amounts in each deal may not be terribly high, but taken all together they form a big enough market, and one that Schnellmann can comfortably keep an eye on. He is not a person who has to react to this market because 'he is the market', as a 1983 article said . The way the market has developed so far is largely due to a fortuitous personal passion. It is not the passion of a gambler, who stakes everything on a number or impulse, but that of a landscape architect or collector who pursues his goal with honest and reliable perseverance.

At the age of 20 he began to collect shares in the same way his friends collected stamps. He used his money to buy shares in mountain railways, and just as a radio ham marks contact with Tahiti, Patagonia or Alaska on his map, Schnellmann took an interest in unknown shares. As one's capital accumulates, it is customary to move on to larger shares, but Schnellmann stuck with his mountain railways. After working for various banks he began making a name for himself in the Willisau Volksbank, some 20 years ago, as the only expert in his field.

Swiss railways have fans throughout the world because of their various different gauges, their strikingly beautiful bridges, their stations with all their local colour and the idyllic landscape. As a child in Japan, I had a book of photographs with just such picturesque images. Even before I got to know Geneva or Zurich, I knew where Grindelwald, Langwies and the Pilatus were. When Schnellmann showed me the table of shares he dealt with, I felt my childhood passion reawake. Just as I had been thrilled by building model trains and making them go, he is thrilled whenever he can put the shares of small mountain railways into circulation. Today, apart from shares in railways, ski-lifts, ferries and hotels, his 'garden' grows shares in local newspapers, electrical shops, textile businesses, breweries and so on. But his greatest passion is still the 110 Alpine railways and the tourist trade that goes with them. For Schnellmann, tourism is one of Switzerland's rewarding areas; this trade, influenced as it is by weather and season, is supported in the long-term by Mr Schnellmann's over-the-counter market.

It is still difficult to acquire information about the shares of small and medium-sized companies except over the telephone, through an announcement in a local paper or by word of mouth. The best way still remains personal contact with the actual businessmen themselves. The difficulty for Schnellmann's role lies on the one hand in the fact that the shares must be brought into circulation in sufficient numbers, and on the other hand that he must know the owners and managers of the companies personally. The market is something like a garden that he has cultivated, in soil that he knows very well. In the middle of the '80s two more banks established divisions for non-admitted shares, and they now deal with around 20 per cent of market transactions. So, it's really a bit of an exaggeration to say that Schnellmann himself constitutes the whole of the market, but it is certainly true to say that his strength lies in his wonderful behind-the-scenes familiarity with all the market movements.

Why are the other banks getting involved at this point? According to Schnellmann advertising was buoyant, the companies were growing and consequently the market was growing as well. Recently, even institutional investors such as insurance companies, pension funds and foundations have begun to take an interest in over-the-counter shares.

The bulk of these shares are traded between banks, and fewer and fewer are being bought by private investors, who are possessed of a collector's mentality which is quite unlike that of the conventional investor, who is chiefly interested in a share's performance. 'Because it's rare, I want it', is the attitude that is required. Schnellmann speaks as one who is convinced by his case and wants to win over more people to his hobby. Even more than his dignity and his fine manners, you sense his confidence that he can reap a comfortable harvest from this field that he has sowed himself. It is more important for him to know the number of Japanese tours to the Jungfraujoch or the snowy peaks of St Moritz than the news from the City or Wall Street. His working method is, of course, 'professional', but just a trace of that 'amateur' atmosphere is still retained.

If these shares are the sea, then this over-the-counter market is a placid harbour in a bay. If a storm should come, it becomes a secure place of refuge. Big waves rolling in from Wall Street or London, whether they are sparkling, sunny ones or threatening, stormy ones, take quite a long time to reach the shore here. The harbour's protective wall absorbs a lot of the shock, so that the surface of the water remains relatively untroubled. In Mr Schnellmann's harbour, the boats are colourful tourist craft. That was my impression of another one of Switzerland's discreet back rooms.

The Alternative Bank, or Banking Ethics

Olten, a town of less than 20,000 inhabitants, does not earn any stars in the Michelin Guide. I was standing on the ground floor of a plain, post-modern building in the Leberngasse. If there had not been a marble plate bearing the inscription 'Alternative Bank' in front of the big window, I am sure I would have mistaken it for a design agency. When I entered, I saw a long-haired man with stubble in a short-sleeved red shirt and jeans working at an open desk, as if in a travel agency. The column behind him was transparent. Part of the wall was painted dark red like a work of art and the gleaming floor-covering was of linoleum, a material with 'eco-logical' qualities. I was invited into Mr Andreas Ragaz' office, where an experimental paint-ing and a small rug from the Andes formed a kind of unit. He too was wearing jeans, and a rough cotton shirt. For him the transparent interior reflects the bank's policy.

After graduating from business school in 1977, Mr Ragaz worked in the credit department of the Swiss Volksbank. He found it difficult to adapt to its ethical and political orientation, or to its military organisation. Directives from above had to be carried out whatever the circum-stances, even if they did not correspond with one's own convictions. The dress-code of the bank's employees (tie, plain shirt, belt with buckle) was not to his liking either. After he had started supporting political opposition to the Army in 1983, he found it impossible to recon-cile the divorce between his lifestyle and that of the bank's and so he left the bank. He then became involved in the planning of an alternative finance company. When this project col-lapsed and German colleagues began to voice criticism and doubts about their alternative banking methods, he came up with the idea of an alternative bank based on realistic con-cepts. The first committee was formed in 1986, including, among others, international organ-isations like Greenpeace. In November 1987 they began to advertise the bank's share-capi-tal, which unexpectedly brought in 9.5 million Swiss francs. Whether it was because they were afraid of putting a blot on their careers, or just simply fear of the risks, people seemed very reluctant to work on the project. The initiators of the idea had no difficulty in getting permis-sion to set up the bank, and preparations went ahead so successfully that they were able to open the offices in Olten in 1990. Olten was chosen for political reasons as well. Although half of the share-holders come from Zurich, they did not want to be confused with the 'gno-mes of Zurich', and anyway, Zurich office rents were too high. In the company prospectus, printed on recycled paper, we are told that the Alternative Bank was opened in the Land of Gnomes and dedicated to the following precepts: 'My money shall make more than interest/ My money shall not support the arms-trade/My money shall not keep the company of fugi-tive money.'

In accordance with these principles, the Alternative Bank (ABS) chiefly supports ecology, organic agriculture, cooperative companies, open schools, feminist initiatives and collabo-rative projects with the Third World. As Dr Peter Bosshard of the 'Berne Declaration', a union of solidarity with the Third World, told me, utopian and 'high-falutin' slogans are no longer able to generate major public debate. Today's pragmatic method seeks to achieve more real-istic goals by the application of professionalism. Mr Ragaz agrees: 'As Swiss citizens we must act in efficient, rational and at the same time ethically correct ways.'

He sees Switzerland as a sort of pirates' 'treasure island', where the money that has flowed in illegally from abroad is buried deep underground. Switzerland itself never had any colonies, says Mr Ragaz, but businessmen and companies expanded, using its neutrality and stability as a selling-point, so that the former colonial powers would go on depositing the money earned in the colonies in Swiss bank accounts. People may be personally opposed to this state of affairs, but it is very difficult to take appropriate action in the professional banking context. Business is business, as they say. The Alternative Bank wants to challenge this attitude. Ethics are the opposite of profit. The ABS has given the matter some thought, because as a bank it depends on getting a return on its investments, but at the same time simply aiming for the maximum return could bring problems. Hence: 'Less money, more sense'. There will always be the problem of deciding where compromise should be made. For Mr Holzach of the Union Bank of Switzerland, it is plain, for example, that a bank cannot condone dealings with a criminal, but it is a different matter if he has repented of his misdeeds and served his sentence. Furthermore: if for some reason there is money that has not been declared to the taxman, that is not the bank's problem, but a problem for the state and the individual in question, and the bank should not be held ethically responsible. At the ABS, on the other hand, loans are granted on the basis of the suppliant's ethical orientation. The Ethical Council and the Ethical Credit Examination Committee are responsible for this. At the moment the ABS is still at the stage of refining its banking practices, but it is certainly the first bank to have dedicated its activities to ethical principle .

Ethical premises were defined for the Swiss banks by Calvin, who was born in Geneva, when he preached that wealth was a reward from God for the select few - something which was not meant for outward show, however, but which should be accumulated privately. Thus the 'spirit' of capitalism emerged from the link between saved capital (= virtue) and continued investments. Economy, efficiency and moderation were thus linked together into an ethic in which this modesty also served to make people wealthier still. Ostentation was to be avoided, even if people felt that they had grown wealthy. Protestantism managed the great feat of acting as an incentive to the efficient and rational exploitation of accumulated capital. Switzerland became a model country in this respect.

All Swiss cities have a reticent style of architecture. Zurich's financial centre does not display its wealth on the Paradeplatz in the demonstrative or overwhelming way Manhattan or Hong Kong do. The restricted height of the buildings has not been compensated for by particularly grandiloquent ornamentation, either. The bank buildings on Zurich's Paradeplatz blend in with the buildings of Sprüngli, Fendi and the Hotel Savoy on the other side of the square. Certainly, the land here is expensive, but the climate of the city could do with more of that special atmosphere, that wind that blows through places like the City of London, the Kabutocho in Tokyo or the Kitahama in Osaka. The utter calm of the city leads many people to think that this peace masks something quite different under the surface.

The Ambivalence of Money is the Ambivalence of Switzerland

In his book *The Philosophy of Money* (1900), the German sociologist Georg Simmel defined capital as something in which the abstract relations of economic value are realized in a concrete substance. As things stand today, we see the numbers flying past on our screens as a kind of value substance. Karl Marx, who was logically, socially and historically even more precise than Simmel, argued that the social expression of wealth stimulates greed; the desire, in other words, to own as much as possible. Anyone can understand greed, more or less, and it is an attribute that is more or less common to everyone. When all of us are young we have the irrational idea that those things that are still hidden and in some way mysterious are the very things that we should consider valuable (Paul Valéry).

Each individual, bearing his own secrets, needs capital in order to be a popular actor on the social stage. But a part of this capital itself wants to be kept secret. Even in an age when wealth passes along global, digitalised electronic circuits the world over, this part cannot be made completely transparent.

Switzerland, which has known the secret of capital since the 15th century, successfully created secret capital - a reprehensible enterprise from a rational point of view. But as long as capital remains capital, there's probably no point in that. As a French philosopher said: 'Money is alive'. Since time immemorial, money has also been linked with sex and dirt (the scarab, which turns dung into gold). In Greek and Assyrian civilization, people were envied for their money, but at the same time there was a mentality that rejected money. Money was sacred and dirty, it brought joy but harboured dangers at the same time.

Bankers, lawyers and doctors are part of the same service industry, but they are never clearly portrayed in films and books. In thrillers and cheap love-stories you find big bankers are generally cast in minor roles; as people opposed to the marriage of a daughter or embroiled in conspiracies. Led astray by evil businessmen and organised crime, the banker is less often a model figure than a perpetrator of evil deeds. At the moment I can think of no play, film or literary work that deals with the normal feelings a banker might have. In fact, in real life, the banker is generally a 'winner'; in fiction, on the other hand, he always appears as a kind of victim. The banker's contradictory popular image reflects the ambiguity of money itself. People may be avaricious, but they do not want to have to touch money themselves.

If Switzerland were to lose its banks, there would be no more safe havens. But there would be a price to pay for this. It could be said that Switzerland has taken upon itself the 'bad conscience' of the capitalist economy. In Switzerland, the positive and rational character of capital is attested to by the punctual, perfect and sober lifestyle, the corollary to which perhaps lies in the intensification of banking secrecy.

Jean-François Bergier makes a striking remark in his *Economic History of Switzerland* which particularly struck me. The myth undoubtedly contains, 'a grain of truth transformed by fantasy'. The stories about the Swiss banks may be fed by fantasy and cliché, but they are not without some foundation. Bergier describes this in the context of the general history of the Swiss banking and does not treat it as a new phenomenon. If we look to the past, we see that in the thirties it was the discretion of the Swiss banks that protected the wealth of Jews by the setting up numbered bank accounts. It was the private banks in Geneva who introduced the principle of discretion which protected the private money flowing in from France and Italy from the prying eyes of the state.

Money did not start flowing into Switzerland with the advent of the international drugs trade, or crises and wars beyond the shores of Europe; well before this, capital had been escaping to Switzerland from war-torn areas of the European continent. Switzerland thus earned a great deal of interest. Twenty-five years ago, Mr Pictet's grandfather told him the following story: 'Time and again, Swiss banks have served, among other things, as the tools of evil. You can make an accusation out of this, but it would be like holding the elephant's tail and saying you had a hold of the whole elephant.' What is certain is that the big drug syndicates and the arms trade are based abroad. Switzerland is often nothing but a deposit box. It is very typical of the country to see itself as being nothing but the tail of the whole business. Does evil come about because there is a secure vault available, or is a vault only necessary because evil exists? The debate is by necessity a circular one.

The secret of the Swiss banks is not their vaults, as such, but the secrecy of a created system within a geographical, political, social, historical and psychological background. In a word, it is the 'nature of Switzerland' or 'Swissness'. But where does discretion stop and secrecy begin? Where does the public sphere end and the private begin? In the shadow of this secrecy there hide dictators, international stars and businessmen who cannot trust their own banks. One thing is clear, and that is that banking secrecy is above mere good and evil. According to Mr Holzach's idea of ethics, a person's criminal activities are their own personal problem and should not affect the bank. Certainly, a dictator is also an individual whose independence and freedom must be protected. But in reality, even if he does not break a single one of his own laws, thousands of people in his own country are born without independence and freedom.

Within Europe, Switzerland acts as an asylum, geographically, politically and economically. Native artists bored by this atmosphere of peace become world famous only when they move to Paris or Berlin. Thus, in the cultural history of Switzerland, you will find more 'big names' among people who stopped off in Switzerland for a while (Richard Wagner, Lenin, James Joyce, Tristan Tzara, Bertold Brecht and Albert Einstein) than 'great Swiss people' themselves. Apparently the inhabitants of other countries need a transit point such as this more than the Swiss themselves. The capital accumulated in Switzerland is reinvested abroad, because the country is much too small to use the accumulated money. In this sense it can quite straightforwardly be called a transit point. The Swiss banks are not only a symbol of world finance, but a veritable symbol of Swiss culture. The French academic Roland Barthes described the Imperial Palace in the centre of Tokyo as a place where the noise of the city is transformed into the peaceful calm of the castle surrounded by its woods. The Imperial Palace is, we might say, a 'place of emptiness' in the sense of being a place of stillness. Switzerland occupies a similar position within Europe.

The Emperor in his castle is not an ordinary citizen. As the supreme patriarch in the Japanese

system, he does not belong to a family either. He seems to be neutral in the Swiss sense. In his seclusion he embodies Japan, drawing his country together as though he were its core and centre. In the same fashion he is the centre of the Shinto religion; this is now the centre of a power without responsibility in political daily life. The Emperor seldom appears in public, but for the social structure and the mentality of the Japanese he is indispensable. Similarly, Switzerland is necessary as a place of asylum – although one that does have responsibilities – for Europe and the world economy. But is there a Switzerland that is necessary for the Swiss themselves?

Little Big Land
Energy and Environment: Equal Parts of the Same Puzzle
Sohan P. Modak

Located at the crossroads of Europe, with an unlimited influx of capital and low interest rates, Switzerland has seen decades of steady growth and prosperity. Not having to face the problem of unemployment so chronic in other western countries, it is not uncommon in Switzerland to hear a heated debate on the balance between the economics of energy and ecological sanity occurring with increasing frequency.

Unlike Scandinavian countries – with their vast land masses, relatively homogeneous ecosystem, low population density and little ethnic and linguistic diversity – Switzerland is split by the Alps into northern and southern zones interspersed with valleys with high population density and considerable ethnic, cultural and linguistic diversity. The mountains pose a formidable barrier and even valleys lying parallel to each other may retain distinct fauna and flora. Seven hundred years after the proclamation of a confederation of sovereign states by Uri, Schwyz and Unterwalden, the cultural diversity is maintained to a large degree. Meanwhile, with the progressive adherence of new territories, Switzerland has grown to 26 cantons and gradually delimited and defined the various authorities, rules and regulations required to deal with issues of common interest through legislative activism within the framework of a confederate democracy. In Switzerland, the executive authority is in the hands of communes and cantons and throughout its modern history one notes a constant tussle between those who want federal laws to ensure the common good and those who refuse to hand over their decentralised executive authority and autonomy in favour of a federated government.

My own perception of Switzerland is coloured by awe and fascination on the one hand and despair on the other: awe for its extraordinary vigour, for the diligence of its citizenry, for its industrial harmony and adaptability in an ever-changing world economic climate, for its ability to hold its position in international financial markets and remain at the forefront of competition; fascination with the innovativeness of its people, with its intelligentsia (including social and natural scientists and technocrats), with its desire to maintain a picture postcard façade with the dedication and precision of an atomic clock; and despair at the notion of Switzerland as a microcosm of an affluent society engaged in the production of incredible wealth and waste through the concerted actions of invisible cartels and private and public monopolies.

This 'little big land' has so many achievements to its credit in science and technology, in land and resource management that it will be interesting to see how it will adapt to changing ecological conditions. Being a small but determined society, the Swiss have adjusted their pace by acting mainly by consensus. Consequently for them, discussing problems and finding their solutions has become an obsession. Yet, despite the extraordinary cultural diversity, the strange admixture and superimposing of religious faith and superstition and the fluid transition from dialect to dialect and from language to language, an original Swiss ethos has indeed emerged from its mountainous terrain. The relatively crisp, though affected, French or German accent in the big cities is tempered by the slow lilt or halting drawl in the countryside and mountains, as if the time taken to say what one wants to say is dictated by the extent of mental unrest.

Every Swiss valley has a different hero, a different focus of cultural pride and worship. Trying to remove the parallax by focusing between the two closest points is already difficult, but to attempt to develop an integrated image of Switzerland for hundreds of different foci is even more difficult. As a student, I sometimes found this diversity so overwhelming that, in the shock of confusion, we used to joke, 'Hey, you got Swissed out!', meaning lost in a sea of possibilities.

Nevertheless, 700 years since its foundation, Switzerland is very much a vibrant reality. Its political system has evolved continuously to a point where it has even prescribed norms to ensure internal fragmentation without destroying the whole (as seen not too long ago with the establishment of the 26th canton, Jura). How does it manage such a diversity? How does it still maintain the image of a peace-loving and picturesque nation? Or, does it really deserve this image? Are Swiss people happy with their socio-economic conditions? Do they still identify with their mountains and rustic countryside, or have they become sufficiently cynical to have manicured them beyond the point of no return? Do the Swiss happen upon a consensus, or is it also forced and then managed? I don't have answers to all these questions and those I have exude unusual ambivalence. Provided with the same information different persons draw diametrically opposite conclusions. The most recent example concerns the choice of nuclear power stations for the production of electricity by power utilities.

This issue has laid bare the direct connection between the politics of energy and the sanity of the environment to such an extent that a debate has raged at all levels – social, economic and political – generating a lasting impact on the environmental consciousness of the man on the street.

The Swiss heart beats to the rhythm of its unique resource, hydroelectricity: 'The strength of a nation is measured by the natural resources it possesses.' This dictum, however, does not apply to Switzerland, whose only natural resource is the water stored and renewed in the form of ice high up in the mountains. The Swiss exploit their water resources to generate electricity which they use themselves and also sell to neighbouring countries. Over 110 streams, rivulets, rivers and their tributaries cascade down the Alps and the Jura to reach the plains. Some join the lakes while others feed into major rivers – the Rhine, the Rhône, the Po and the Inn – originating in and coursing out of Switzerland. Between the end of the 19th century and 1910, 28 hydroelectricity-generating plants were installed with a total water capacity of 400 million cubic metres producing two billion kw/hours of electricity annually. By 1985, with more than 1,000 units, this capacity increased 16 times to 11,670 MW, producing 32 billion kw/hours which still accounted for only 60 per cent of all electricity produced in Switzerland, the remaining 40 per cent being produced in four nuclear power plants.

Nuclear power plants generate electricity continuously and the power production cannot be adjusted to the daily cycle of electricity consumption. By contrast, hydropower plants can be shut down or activated within minutes by controlling the flow of water to the turbines. Hydroelectricity producers adjust their generating schedules to match the prime period with high demand. In the early days, water accumulated in dams and barrages was channelled down to the turbines to produce power, and then flowed out downstream. Switzerland was thus producing excess electricity early in winter and less later on toward midsummer. With the availability of a continuous stream of nuclear power, and a subsequent control over hydroelectricity during the peak demand period, the production life of the water reservoirs increased somewhat, but the water gushing down through the turbines is lost permanently to the reservoir, so that Switzerland still has to import electricity during late winter and early summer. A full water reservoir is like a full accumulator or a fully charged battery which, once empty, has to be recharged by water from melting glaciers during summer. Since the electricity produced during prime time commands higher rates than that produced during periods of low demand, Swiss engineers had the ingenious idea of buying cheap electricity produced at night to pump water back into the high dams or secondary storage tanks. This water can then be allowed to gravitate towards the turbines again when required, to produce more 'prime time' electricity. A number of Swiss power utilities have now adopted this mode of operation, thereby either prolonging the period of hydroelectricity generation, or increasing the power output during the peak period.

One of the most elaborate organisations of this type is to be found at Oberhasli in the Bernese Oberland, run by the Bernese Power Utility Co. The Oberhasli-Grimsel complex contains a series of barrages, artificial high-altitude storage tanks for repumping water, and an elaborate system of underground tunnels and power plants. Since the repumping operation proved highly profitable, the utility company planned on further augmenting the water storage capacity of the main Grimsel-West reservoir project from 200 million cubic metres to 500 million cubic metres. In Switzerland, all construction project proposals are first put to public hearing, enquiry and scrutiny, and it soon became evident that the augmented reservoir would partly submerge the main glacier and endanger the rare alpine species in its vicinity.

From 1985 on, Swiss ecologists, members of the Swiss section of the World Wildlife Fund, the Swiss Foundation for Landscape Protection and Management and other organisations mounted a synchronised offensive against the project by inundating the commission of enquiry with 500-600 counterdepositions. Environmentalists have adopted an increasingly militant stance by denouncing the desire for increased profitability by power utilities at the cost of precious natural heritage and wildlife. Their arguments are clear: With the hydroplants, forest management and maintenance of grazing pastures, the real land mass clothed by natural forests and glaciers is decreasing alike so that no further encroachment should be tolerated. The Grimsel-West project quickly got bogged down and has been contested so hotly to date that the coming years promise a great divide between ecologists and power utilities.

Surprisingly, another monumental project at the Grand Dixence – which boasts the tallest barrage in Europe of 285 metres and a 100 km-long system of collecting tunnels – somehow got clearance, the project director's justification being that the existing barrage is like a Rolls Royce run on a two horsepower motor. The Sfr 1 billion plan therefore involves the construction of an additional system of underground tunnels and a massive power plant to augment the power production from its present 700 MW to 2,000 MW. Not much is said about the fact that in order to fill such giant reservoirs, water from a number of nearby valleys must be tapped, collected and diverted. Often in such cases, the land dries up, affecting the naturally protected habitats of the wildlife. In any case, the Swiss are more energy-hungry and more wasteful than others in relation to their energy wealth. With electricity consumption increasing at an annual average rate of 2.3 per cent, much concern is being expressed about how to cope with the demand. The pressure from ecologists is also mounting to save the last bastions of unspoilt landscape and unmanicured wilderness from the onslaught of electricity utilities. With many organisations such as WWF (World Wildlife Fund), SL (Swiss Foundation for Landscape Protection and Management), Heimatschutz (Heritage Protection Association), and Naturschutz (Swiss League for Nature Protection) now on their toes, considerable public opinion is being generated against any further encroachment on the wildlife, wilderness and scenic heritage.

The Nuclear Option

In 1957, Swiss people approved the initiative for 'peaceful use of nuclear energy and protection against radiation', thereby paving the way for the installation of nuclear power stations. With the possibilities being very limited both for the construction of new hydro-plants, and for the augmentation of output from existing ones, the use of 'clean' or 'pollution-free' nuclear energy seemed attractive – a favourable alternative to thermal plants fired by fossil fuels. Thus here, like elsewhere in the world, the man on the street was not well informed, nor were the nuclear engineers and experts fully accustomed to estimating the nature and extent of the hazard represented by nuclear power plants. With reactor technology itself in its infancy, it was not possible to estimate the integrated impact of a plant malfunction on the environment. Engineers the world over are a law unto themselves and think that all problems can be preempted or solved by an appropriate technological fix. No wonder Michael Kohn, the 'father' of four out of the nine proposed nuclear power plants, was much saddened by the negative attitude of public opinion towards nuclear power generation in Switzerland. He says, 'Out of my four children, two, including Kaiseraugst, died prematurely, while two others – Gösgen and Leibstadt – survived to do well.' The first three reactors with a 1,020 MW capacity – Beznau I, II, and Mühleberg – were established between 1970 and 1972.

While the long-term perspective of human history is predictable, its short-term flashes and fish-tailing are not. The intense involvement, turmoil and defeat of the uprisings of May 1968 left a lot of wounds on the young generation committed to instituting an alternative to the established ruling forces of both Left and Right. Looking for another cause – beyond the struggle against the tyranny of the military-industrial complex denounced by the American activists, beginning with the Berkeley protests and their anti-Vietnam sentiments – the players soon regrouped under the anti-nuclear banner. One of the first such regroupings began in and around Basle to include the local Swiss, as well as the French and German activists, who had attacked the proposal to construct the nuclear power plant at Kaiseraugst. By 1973, a Nonviolent Action Group Against Kaiseraugst was established. The members occupied the proposed construction site in 1975, organised a massive march to Berne in 1977, and participated in the completion of a requisite signature-gathering campaign for a popular referendum against the installation of nuclear power plants. Between 1972 and 1977, the anti-nuclear protests spread to other proposed sites in Gösgen, Graben, Inwil, Leibstadt, Rüthi and Verbois. Despite all this, at Gösgen and Leibstadt reactors were established in 1979 and 1984 respectively, adding another 1,900 MW to the electricity-generating capacity and increasing the total share of nuclear plants to 40 per cent of the total electricity produced in Switzerland.

The commissioning of the Gösgen plant is particularly interesting as it coincided with the disaster at the Three Mile Island nuclear plant in the U.S. To date, all five reactors at the four sites in Switzerland have shown a fault-free operation. One by one, other sites have dropped out of contention. Kaiseraugst generated the most political heat and environmental awakening among the population. Anti-nuclear became the cause célèbre of the young and the bête noire of the industrialists, investors and politicians. The article for the first popular anti-nuclear referendum stipulated that the people in the vicinity of the site of a proposed nuclear plant should have the right to agree to or to reject the construction. In one of the closest votes in Swiss history with almost 50 per cent of the electorate voting, the referendum was lost by a knife-edge margin.

Licking their wounds, anti-nuclear lobbyists regrouped and two more initiatives were put to the vote in 1984. The first article asked for a total ban on the construction of nuclear power stations after the completion of Leibstadt, while the second emphasised the development of other renewable and clean sources of energy, along with energy conserving measures. Again, both initiatives lost in the popular vote by a small margin. Every aspect of the voting pattern and final results were analysed by both groups. The subsequent spate of industrial disasters – Bhopal (1984), Schweizerhalle (1986) and the deadly explosion at the Chernobyl nuclear power plant in the USSR (1986) – was too much for the Swiss populace. Ecologists regrouped and developed a committed membership to rekindle popular sentiment against the construction of nuclear power stations. The post-Chernobyl ticking of Geiger counters in the hilly parts of the Jura and southern Switzerland and the release of highly toxic pesticides into the Rhine from the fire at Sandoz' Schweizerhalle plant caused even the pro-nuclear skeptics to make an about-turn, and a third initiative to abandon nuclear energy completely – to which two more initiatives were added, to observe a ten-year moratorium on nuclear plant construction and to conserve energy as well as seeking alternative energy sources – was launched in 1987.

In 1987, a massive and contentious study was published by the Expert Group Energy Scenario (EGES) commissioned by the Federal Council which led to the grouping of the Greens, environmentalist organisations such as WWF, SL and the Left on the one side, and the big capital and electricity-producing cartel on the other. This report was directed not only at electricity production but also at the development of alternative energy sources and conservation measures, including the development of energy-efficient devices. Furthermore, the EGES proposed a novel 'carrot or stick' method: an Eco Bonus for those who conserved energy and a taxation penalty for those who wasted it. Perhaps the most important contribution of the EGES was its estimation of the real social costs of energy production and utilisation. In my discussions with a wide variety of representatives of both pro- and anti-nuclear groups, one of the surprising findings was that Switzerland did not have, until very recently, a national energy policy. The development and exploitation of energy had always been entirely left up to free market forces. Therefore the EGES document is the precursor for a rational energy policy.

During the past two centuries, many of the attempts made to protect the countryside, the mountains and the scenic heritage against encroachment and pollution by modern industrial society had led to the establishment of a series of laws, as well as a clear policy statement, relating to environmental protection. By contrast, until the enactment of the Energy Ordinance which became effective on 1 May 1991, no legislation regulating energy affairs existed. Even the Federal Office of Energy, a recent creation for studying energy-related matters, is devoid of any regulatory powers.

The trials and tribulations of the nuclear option generated a real sense of concern for environmental responsibility among Swiss people. Questions were also raised about civil responsibility in case of disaster. Even more important was the debate generated in the search for alternative sources of energy. If the demand for electricity is increasing by 2.3 per cent annually, where will the additional output come from? Should Switzerland depend on imports from French nuclear power utilities, or even Eastern Europe? Or should one develop alternative sources? Michael Kohn is right in pointing out that it is hypocritical for a committed anti-nuclear activist to agree on the importation of nuclear power from abroad. In 1988, the pro-nuclear lobby suddenly withdrew from the Kaiseraugst project and received compensation for their investment in the project. In the vote on 23 September 1990, the Swiss population showed extraordinary wisdom in defeating the initiative which advocated the complete banning and phasing-out of nuclear power, and, at the same time, accepting a ten-year moratorium on any new construction of nuclear power plants. Thus, on the one hand, the nuclear power industry was being challenged to come up with fail-safe power plants while, on the other, the supporters of the 'alternative' were being pushed to demonstrate the feasibility of viable, renewable energy sources and systems to meet the increased annual demand. The voters also gave teeth to the federal government to introduce an energy tax and Eco Bonus in a twofold action for energy conservation.

In 1991, the Federal Council introduced an ordinance for the economical and rational use of energy that prescribed standards for the utilisation of energy by vehicles, home appliances and the estimation of the efficiency of water and house-heaters; to support those who produce their own electricity which can then be fed into the national grid; and to promote the efficient use of energy by developing new technologies, pilot plants, demonstrations, research, heat-recovery systems and renewable sources of energy. The ordinance also stipulates an important reduction in carbon dioxide emission. This is perhaps one of the most sweeping sets of regulations governing energy matters to be adopted anywhere in the world. This positive development resides in the commitment to accelerated research and development of alternative sources of energy. Clearly, the alternative sources cannot be expected to replace the existing systems completely, but any attempt to develop and promote renewable energy sources would lead to 'value-added' returns.

Alternative Renewable Sources of Energy

The non-polluting and renewable sources of energy include sun, wind, bio-gas and tides, in addition to hydropower. In Switzerland, hydroelectricity power production has already peaked and can only be minimally increased. The moratorium on nuclear power plants has ensured that unless draconian measures are introduced for energy conservation, nuclear power will have to be imported in increasing quantities from, say, France. Indeed, the electricity distribution consortia have already signed contracts to ensure the importations until the year 2025. The Federal Office of Energy estimates that it will take between ten and 30 years to generate meaningful amounts of solar energy. Fossil fuels pollute, while wind-power potential is small and geographically limited. The existing solar technology which uses photovoltaic panels gives about twelve per cent conversion to electricity and the capital costs are almost ten times that of conventional power generation, however, it is likely that the spheral solar technology developed in the U.S. will lead to a fivefold decrease in capital costs. Professor Pierre Fornallaz of the Langenbruck Centre for Ecology argues that although a solar unit costs Sfr 0.35 as compared to Sfr 0.09 for a nuclear unit, the real cost of production and clean-up for other energy sources has not been rationally calculated and included in the cost to the consumer. For example, the price of petrol is one franc per litre while the total costs inclusive of the clean-up of pollution is estimated at six francs. This extraordinary discrepancy is real and led to the suggestion of introducing an Eco Bonus for reducing car mileage and improving the efficiency of heating installations using electricity or fossil fuels. In Switzerland, electricity accounts for only 20-25 per cent of the total energy used, while fossil fuels account for the rest used by factories, house-heating, vehicles and so on.

The conceptual framework for integrated, decentralised power generation and networking, or the 'interconnection' proposed by Prof. Fornallaz, gives real hope for the rational production and use of energy. Quite simply, install a solar panel, or a windmill, or both; optimise the heat exchange by modifying the exposed faces of the house; achieve efficient heat transfer by using a Stirling motor; improve the insulation of house windows and doors; opt for home appliances operating at a lower wattage and install low-wattage lighting; if fea-

sible, install a bio-gas plant. Thus, after domestic use, there will remain a small excess of power which can then be fed – at a price – into the national grid, the idea being to reduce the energy deficit appreciably. After all, with a continuous on-stream production of electricity by nuclear plants, the hydroelectricity producers have cleverly adapted their production schedules to the peak demand period, thus practically doubling their income. And so, on sunny days, photovoltaic panels would do just that, and so would windmills and bio-gas plants, although to a lesser extent. It is not surprising that pro-nuclears often happen to own shares in electricity cartels and distribution companies and scoff at the idea. In any case, whether or not auto-producers will ever actually manage to produce enough power to feed into the national grid, their right to do so is now guaranteed by ordinance.

At present, however, there exist too many misunderstandings and impediments in the way of any meaningful introduction of nonconventional energy. A notable energy expert brushed off solar panels as a nuisance, saying, 'I don't want to look down the valley from my hilltop villa and get back a flash of light reflected by a rooftop solar panel.' Exactly the same argument is presented by some of the associations vigilant in the protection of landscapes and heritage. Couldn't the same energy expert think of using glare-free glass to cover the panels? Has the Heritage Protection Association taken a firm stand against the littering of the beautiful Swiss countryside with ugly, gaudily painted industrial sheds, factories and warehouses which are eyesores for anyone travelling by road or rail? If you travel on the Japanese bullet train, it is astonishing to note that practically every rooftop has a solar panel, which in no way affects the scenery. Japan, too, has practically no natural resources, and the Japanese countryside is no less picture postcard-like than that of Switzerland. Indeed, why not make the installation of solar panels compulsory for all industrial establishments, and commercial and residential sectors?

The bio-gas alternative is probably at its most neglected and poorly developed in Switzerland. At Infra-Solar in Tänikon, the picture is gloomy. Out of over 10,000 farms, there are only 150 bio-gas plants in Switzerland. The real reason is the prohibitive cost of installation. To be viable, a bio-gas plant should be operated with ten cattle units: one unit is equivalent to one cow, one bull, or seven pigs, and a Swiss farmer is allowed to rear three cattle units per hectare, for which he is entitled to receive a subsidy of Sfr 3,500 per unit. At Tänikon, I was told, the estimated cost of a bio-gas plant is Sfr 3,000 per cattle unit. A farmer, therefore, would be required to spend Sfr 30-40,000 for a profitable operation. This cost estimate compares with Sfr 1,500 for the same plant in India! Again, the price-fixing in Switzerland would be enough to kill any concept. In the Canton of Lucerne, the regulation governing the number of cattle units is routinely violated: the farmer may own as many as 80 pigs or eleven cattle units per hectare. As a result, the pig urine and manure has created one of the most serious pollution problems in the lakes; quite a large part of the problem could have been dealt with by encouraging these farmers to use bio-gas plants.

Switzerland is a land of cartels (about 1,200) which control the national economy and pricing practices, especially on imported goods. The real difficulty will have to be faced in making renewable propositions which are viable alternatives to these cartels. After all, every basic amenity is two to four times more expensive than in surrounding countries. The system operates through a multilayered, cascading subsidy on the one hand and liberal price-fixing by the cartels on the other. Naturally for the cartels, joining a unified Europe will be a very painful exercise as their hold on the commodity markets, finance, agricultural production, the labour market, power utilities and so on, would be quickly lost.

In any case, due to massive cross ownership, and government and private institutional collaboration, the owners themselves appear to be giving away power to the people or auto-producers. With practically all European nations connected to a common grid, those who control the transfer points on the international grid control the energy economics of that nation. In Switzerland, the transfer points are owned by Elektrowatt SA, a subsidiary of Swiss Credit Bank. Elektrowatt also owns shares in many power utilities and distribution networks to constitute, along with Motor Columbus, ABB and Sulzer, as well as with most communes and cantons, the ownership of the electricity cartel.

The Environment

Calamities and catastrophes have existed since time immemorial, but they have become more and more frequent. The 18th century was marked by huge avalanches and landslides. The relationship between frequent catastrophes and human activity becomes evident when one considers that more and more forest land has been converted to agriculture and grazing pastures. Intensive tree-felling and deforestation has caused erosion, landslides, and has changed the course of mountain streams and rivers. As they reached the foothills, the rivers constantly changed direction, and the riverbeds turned to marshlands. Just as deforestation affected the flora and fauna, so did the rapid generation of marshlands cause further modification in the flora and fauna. Marshy valleys became breeding grounds for pests, and insect-borne diseases like malaria became rampant. In his treatise, *Les Suisses et l'Environnement*, François Walter traces the causal relationship between human activity and ecological degradation in Switzerland. Some of the cases are spectacular and allow a better understanding of this relationship. For example, a brilliant feat of environmental engineering was to take up and complete the correction of the course of the river Linth in order to eliminate the marshlands. Not only was this achieved rapidly but, by the end of the 19th century, the courses of all the major rivers had been corrected. This not only eliminated the marshlands but also caused a dramatic reduction in the number of pests and the creation of new farmlands with rich alluvial soil in the valleys. Within a hundred years or so high altitude agriculture was shifted down to the valleys and, except in the areas of grazing pastures, mountain forests re-emerged. Drastic change in the ecosystem has also been detrimental to flora and fauna. At the present time, WWF-Switzerland lists that out of 362 vertebrate species, 35 became extinct and 182 are near-extinct or endangered. Similarly, 863 out of 1,856 recorded insect species, and 864 out of 2,691 plant species, are either extinct or endangered. Among vertebrates, for example, fish such as the river lampray, sturgeon and the Atlantic salmon, mammals such as the wild dog and brown bear, and birds such as the red partridge, are extinct. The lynx was reintroduced recently but is still in a precarious state. With the reduction in carnivores, the population of ungulates has increased dramatically, causing a serious disequilibrium which is threatening the forests.

With the advent of industrialisation and intensive agriculture, land, air and water resources are equally menaced. The situation has improved only through a progressive enactment of laws to regulate air and water pollution. For example, the treatment of sewage waste water was made compulsory, and today 95 per cent of all civic waste water is cleaned in treatment plants, such as the huge complexes in Werdhölzli in Zurich, and released in potable water condition into the rivers and lakes. Laws against the discharge of industrial wastes into rivers and water bodies are more or less adhered to. However, the main culprit – agricultural waste – remains.

The case in point is that of Lake Sempach, and other nearby lakes in the Cantons of Lucerne and Aargau. No major river drains into Lake Sempach, nor does any water leave it, except by evaporation. The farmers around this area engage in intensive pig-rearing and flout the federal regulation regarding the number of cattle units permitted per hectare: the actual value in this area is ten to eleven cattle units as opposed to the allowable number of three. Worse still, the intensive pig-farming results in the production of huge quantities of pig urine and faeces which, along with agricultural fertilisers, are washed by rain into the lake, causing extreme eutrophication. Lake Sempach was eutrophicated to the point where most fish species died out. Furthermore, the blue-green alga, Alphanizomeum flosaquae, flourished, and the toxin excreted by this alga killed 400,000 fish in 1984 alone. A visionary experiment in environmental engineering was undertaken by Dr Stadelmann of the Water Resources Office of the Canton of Lucerne in collaboration with ETH in Zurich: pure liquified oxygen is released through a rotating carousel placed at the bottom of the lake over four years ago. They now find a dramatic improvement in the reduction of soluble phosphorous and ammonia with a concommitant reduction in the levels of eutrophication, gradual restitution of the white fish population and reduction in the growth of the blue-green alga. However, the experiment does not decrease the levels of nitrates, which must be achieved by strictly applying the existing regulation on the number of pigs to be reared per hectare, installing bio-gas plants and reducing the use of chemical fertilisers.

During my discussions with various experts, a surprising but significant finding was that women are not involved to the same extent as men in ecological activism. With full voting rights granted to all Swiss women only just last year, the situation reflects the personal bias of the players in the field. It is most surprising that men are unable to appreciate the extent of insight and management capabilities that women possess in eco-logistics. Women are always closest to the action in the cycle of consumption and are the fondest inheritors of the principle of recycling as an unquestioned value. Thus, the failure of Swiss men to incorporate the advice, opinion and full participation of women also contributes to the male-dominated ecological disequilibrium.

Many problems exist, many have been recognised and some have been solved. But the environmental puzzle is like a can of worms: the wider you open it; the more creatures crawl out. There exists in Switzerland so much expertise on the nature of the malady which has been inflicted on the environment by pollution that a concerted and wilful collaboration on the part of the Swiss could avert the environmental disaster and place Switzerland at the forefront of a world trying to recover from the shock and ravages of mismanaged industrialisation. The same is true for the problems of energy equilibrium. After all, energy and the environment are two sides of the same coin, or two interlocking pieces of the same puzzle. Wouldn't it be wonderful if environmental experts, representatives of WWF, SL and Greenpeace, energy experts from the Swiss hautes écoles and an equal number of female experts came together with the clear objective of bringing sanity, scholarship and cool-headed management into the exercise of increasing the face value of the eco-energy tangle! It would be the best gift that Switzerland could offer to Homo sapiens on the occasion of the 700th anniversary. A nation that has built the longest tunnels, successfully undertaken the most complex water and land management projects, invented the rack railway and built the best solar-powered automobile (the Spirit of Bienne) cannot lose. Surely a nation that can return the water sullied by life processes in a clean state to Nature can also give up its ethno-socio-economic-linguistic differences to restore the ecological balance. In any case, the stage is set in Switzerland for a dramatic socio-political greening. An opinion poll conducted by the magazine *L'Illustré* in 1991 amply demonstrates that not only is the local population concerned about the serious degradation of the environment, but it is becoming increasingly disposed toward the need for rapid corrective measures. To succeed, however, the Swiss will have to leave their cars at home and conserve energy at the cost of reduced exposure of their fancy wares.

Beyond the Matterhorn: Redefining Swiss Tourism
Carol Thatcher

The Swiss pioneered the way for others in tourism by inventing a new superior standard of hospitality which won them the accolade 'hotel keepers to kings and kings of hotel keepers.' That was a reputation they enjoyed nearly a century ago, but, hand-in-hand with the growth of a mature tourism industry, there has developed a dilemma controversially articulated by Professor Jost Krippendorf, formerly of Berne University: 'The Swiss want to attract tourists but they would prefer that they stay at home. The best thing would be for them to send the money and not come.' Krippendorf's comment is symptomatic of a complete turnabout in attitude in a country where tourism is the third largest contributor to the nation's exports after machinery, industries and chemicals. In the wide-ranging debate on where tourism in Switzerland is going, all views – both moderate and radical – between these parameters are being exhaustively argued and discussed by the Swiss.

On paper, Switzerland's image as a destination for potential visitors appears to be the almost perfectly orchestrated success story. An introduction to the country in one major guidebook reads: 'Switzerland remains an ideal country to visit, and for a variety of excellent reasons. It is exceedingly comfortable, with a bewildering range of fine hotels and restaurants in all price ranges. It is remarkably beautiful, with an astonishing range of landscapes: alpine peaks, rolling meadows, mirror–like lakes, richly historic towns and cities.'

This thoroughly complimentary passage must come close to inflicting such an inferiority complex on competitors chasing a slice of the lucrative international tourist market that they graciously concede defeat and retire from the business altogether. Yet they don't, and, paradoxically, the fact that Switzerland is a marathon veteran in the tourism arena is both a strength and a weakness. It benefits from the reflected glory, proven form and excellent infrastructure of having been a past champion and an enormous repeat business makes up the core of its visitor statistics. But it is vulnerable to the relentless pressure applied by younger contenders energetically sprinting past, brandishing temptingly trendy holiday options.

Switzerland's international image is one of a miniature spotless 'Heidi–land' in the heart of Europe, whose national industries are manufacturing watches, chocolate and cheese with built-in holes, where little happens to raise the blood pressure and trains run with stopwatch punctuality. The irony is that the new countries making their tourism debuts crave to have even half as clearly defined an international profile as Switzerland's – symbolised by posters of tinkling cowbells around the necks of contented cows grazing in lush green emerald meadows against a backdrop of snowy alpine peaks – while the Swiss wince at this set-in-concrete illusion as a cliché which works against their efforts to present a broader perception of themselves.

The reality convinces visitors that Switzerland has enough versatility to entice them back again and again. Part of the draw must be the composite connotations of what is Swiss in a country which doesn't have one national language but four – Swiss-German, French, Italian and Romansh. This, combined with its geographical location, means that Switzerland is more 'European' in many ways than her five neighbours (Germany, France, Austria, Liechtenstein and Italy). According to Walter Leu, head of the Swiss National Tourist Office (SNTO) which promotes the country worldwide, the average tourist has been there at least five times before, a gratifyingly high proportion by any yardstick. I am one of them, and declare an immediate bias in that I have been captivated by Switzerland and the Alps since I learned to ski in Lenzerheide as a child of eight. Even today, the first aerial picture postcard view of the snowcapped, toothy Alps from an aeroplane window as it approaches Geneva renews my love affair with the country every time.

I've always been rather thrilled by the consummate ease with which it is possible to yo-yo from Switzerland into the next door countries. On a simplistic level (but one close to my heart as an avid skier), it makes it exceedingly easy when skiing in Zermatt to enjoy genuine Italian pasta for lunch – just head down the eight-kilometre Ventina run (registering how incredibly different the Matterhorn looks from behind) to Cervinia, which is in Italy. I find it remarkable that a country 220 kms N/S and 348 kms E/W can sandwich such physical and cultural diversity within its borders. Scarcely a fifth of the 1,000-km-long alpine range is in Switzerland (the French fume that the Swiss have successfully cultivated the myth that Mont Blanc – Europe's highest mountain – is theirs when it is in France) and only half of the country is strictly mountainous. That portion includes over one hundred 4,000 metre summits of the Alps and it is this halo of peaks which dominates the whole Swiss tourism scene as totally as the Grand Canyon dictates that of Arizona.

From Saas Fee – dubbed the 'pearl of the Alps' because it sits in a dramatic horseshoe of mountains – and car-free Zermatt – towered over by the Matterhorn whose angular silhouette is one of the country's most immediately recognisable symbols – there is a treasure trove of summits, ridges, pinnacles and spectacular formations which moved Lord Byron to describe them as 'palaces of nature.' Europe's great rivers have their sources in these mountains, but landlocked Switzerland's nearest ocean point is the Italian seaport of Genoa, 250 kms to the south on the Mediterranean. Keen sailors will not be disappointed in Switzerland though, because anywhere in the country they're barely more than 15 kms from a lake. Geneva and Constance at 250 sq kms qualify as mini-seas, with shorelines studded with sailing marinas packed with mast and riggings at straw-in-a-haystack density.

The variety Switzerland encompasses can be under-appreciated and will always be epitomised for me by the instance where, one morning, I took off from Geneva in the kind of miserable rainy March weather that the city usually reserves for United Nations summits and discovered on landing in Lugano that I had fast-forwarded into Ticino's warm Latin spring. I joined a cosmopolitan mix of Italians, Germans and Swiss relaxing at open air cafés in sun-drenched Ascona, outside Locarno on Lake Maggiore. Ski fanatics eked out their farewell descents of the season on nearby slopes before the snow melted, while we smugly sipped aperitifs knowing we had stolen a headstart on summer.

Being a compact little country with a model transit system, Switzerland is tailor-made for the independent traveller. Choose between rolling along 71,000 kms of impeccable, blissfully uncongested roads or let the train take the strain over 5,000 kms of track and enjoy being a passenger on one of the world's best-run rail systems. Probably the classic journey is the Glacier Express from Zermatt to St. Moritz. It takes a romantic seven and a half hours through a visual feast of high-rise scenery. A second is up to the Jungfraujoch (at 3,475 metres, Europe's highest train station) way above the Bernese Oberland resorts of Wengen and Grindelwald, reached by a track bored through the North Face of the Eiger. Most visitors are divided as to whether to admire more the courageous civil engineering expertise which completed the line in 1912, or the awesome beauty of the 23-km-long Aletsch glacier. From the observation terrace the view is guaranteed to make vertigo sufferers giddy – it used to be the privilege of steely-nerved mountaineers only, the richly earned reward for having so dangerously inched up there.

And now you can commute in civilised Swiss comfort the whole way up! Of the half a million sightseers a year who make the trip, many only arrive in Switzerland hours before – perhaps in Geneva off the high-speed train from Paris, three hours away. Some are in perpetual motion and dash through so fast 'doing Europe' that they send their photographs back to Switzerland asking what they have snapped! It's all a very different tempo from Queen Victoria, who recorded her impressions of lovely Lucerne with a paintbrush, attracted by the same powerful allure of the Swiss Alps and lakes. It was in becoming, over a century ago, a fashionable oasis for royalty and for the intellectual and cultural luminaries of the Romantic Movement that Switzerland was able to begin marketing its unique Alpine grandeur more widely. At this time, Swiss infrastructure was already enviably advanced, and included an efficient railway system boasting tunnels through the Alps as early as the St. Gotthard in 1882 and the Simplon in 1906, and a famous reputation as hosts established by legendary hoteliers like the Seiler family in Zermatt, the Badrutts in St. Moritz, and Caesar Ritz. Swiss was synonymous with the best in international circles when travel was the privilege of the elite. Richard Wagner came to compose, William Turner to paint, Johann Wolfgang von Goethe and John Ruskin to visit. Mark Twain's enthusiasm is evident in ' A Tramp Abroad' and Lord Byron was sufficiently inspired to wax lyrical:

Clear, placid Leman! thy contrasted lake,
With the wild world I dwelt in, is a thing
Which warns me, with its stillness, to forsake
Earth's troubled waters for a purer spring.

Eighteenth century British traveller Samuel Butler was so enchanted by the Garden of Eden-like beauty of the Italian-speaking canton of Ticino that he was too overwhelmed for words, and instead jotted down a few bars of Handel's Messiah. At a less exalted level, but one which captures the spell the Alps cast on the first adventurous visitors, are excerpts from a diary kept by a Miss Jemima Morrell who went on Thomas Cook's inaugural conducted tour of Switzerland in 1863 (he was variously hailed as the patron saint of travel and the Napoleon of excursions). Miss Morrell vividly communicates her effervescent excitement. 'But on making a turn in the road we are – shall I say petrified or paralysed? Neither, but thrown into an arrested state of mental temperament which those extreme expressions physically denote, as unexpectedly the valley of the Rhone, one of *the* views of the Alps is, like a mirage, unrolled before us. Oh! gentle reader [why are readers always supposed to be gentle?] that your retina could be enamelled with the grandeur of that matchless landscape.'

In common with many of today's holiday-makers who prefer their secret hideaways to remain just that, there existed fans of the early alpine cult who abhorred the idea of their beloved mountains being on the general tourist beat. John Ruskin was one who vehemently condemned the fledgling organised travel business, in words which have a prophetic ring: 'The French revolutionaries made stables of the cathedrals of France; you have made race-courses of the cathedrals of the earth. Your one conception of pleasure is to drive in railroad carriages round their aisles, and eat off their altars... [There is no] foreign city in which the spread of your presence is not marked among its fair old streets and happy gardens by a consuming white leprosy of new hotels... The Alps themselves, which your own poets used to love so reverently, you look upon as soaped poles in a bear garden, which you set yourself to climb and slide down again with 'shrieks of delight.'

Ruskin excepted, the British can claim a portion of the credit for initially launching Swiss winter tourism. A party of 16 British and American guests spent the winter of 1864 at Johannes Badrutt's Kulm Hotel in St. Moritz. They skated on the lake, hurtled downhill on toboggans and honed the skills they would later test on the tortuous bends of the Cresta Run – and thus the Engadine Valley was born as a snowy vacation venue. The following summer a fellow Englishman, Edward Whymper, conquered the Matterhorn, which came to symbolise virgin alpine beauty during the turn of the century on posters like Emil Cardinaux's 1908 classic in which it appears boldly depicted in fireball orange.

Other posters of the time indicate the nature of Swiss tourism in that halcyon era – it was the ultimate quality version for the elite and generated generous revenue for its country without any of the cultural and social disadvantages associated with present-day Switzerland. Switzerland as a destination then conjured up images of palatially grand hotels – at the beginning of this century, the country already had three-quarters the number of today's hotel beds – veritable Victorian turreted edifices in Montreux, Lucerne, Interlaken and the island of Brissago in Lake Maggiore.

Montreux was selected by the Russian aristocracy as a winter retreat. They journeyed there on their own trains accompanied by extravagant entourages including private armies which trained with Swiss soldiers during their stay. Social activity in Montreux was a whirl of chandeliers and tiaras, and the cultural life supported a total of nine theatres; it all echoed the style of Cannes and Nice, in the twilight of a period whose days were numbered – by the countdown to the outbreak of war in 1914.

When Europe started to grind back to life in peacetime after two wars, new factors were transforming the travel scene. Initially Switzerland capitalised on being an oasis in battle-ravaged Europe, and Lucerne became so fabled a vacation spot for holidaying American

GI's stationed in war-torn Germany that half a century later a poll in one prestigious US glossy travel publication still rated it among the world's top ten tourist cities.

Then the spectre of mass tourism started to have an impact and Switzerland found itself facing serious competition from an increasing array of choices offered by countries launching themselves on the international holiday market in a world newly shrunk by jet travel. These novice tourist nations frequently had subsidised investment from their governments and quickly mastered the art of building fancy hotels which served drinkable coffee and were efficiently run – ironically often staffed by Swiss graduates of the world-renowned Ecole Hôtelière in Lausanne – founded in 1893 – fanning out across the globe to form a hotel managers 'mafia'.

Affluent Europeans – the Swiss themselves quickly becoming some of the most avid travellers per capita of population – discovered long-haul travel and took to the pleasures of ambitiously vacationing in Kenya, Bali, Acapulco and the Caribbean. They eschewed hiking in the Grisons for trekking in the Himalayas, discovered alternative lakes to their own, and stayed on houseboats in Kashmir, or in Indian island palaces. Switzerland, which guaranteed a hassle-free holiday as surely as there is a gadget on a Swiss Army knife to open anything and everything, seemed dull and boring in comparison to the sexiness and excitement promised by the new destinations. Travel and where you spent your holidays acquired a social cachet – it mattered in the kudos count along with the neighbourhood you lived in, the restaurants you patronised, the car you drove. There was a rush among trendsetters to go to the latest, 'hottest', most exotic island/jungle/safari 'find' to come onto the market. Off the beaten track was in vogue and traditional Switzerland looked too run-of-the-mill, too conventionally manicured. It is feasible to argue that it was not Switzerland itself which had changed intrinsically, rather it was the taste of this new holidaying public that shifted from getting away from it all to getting to where it would all be turned on.

Rest and recreation surrounded by beautiful scenery were usurped as essential holiday ingredients by a suddenly obligatory entertainment element. Peace and tranquillity on a beach or by a lake was no longer enough – there had to be additional manufactured commercial paraphernalia like beach bars, sea scooters for hire, water skiing, paragliding on tap, glass-bottomed boats for tourist trips to view the coral reefs. Massive purpose-built resort 'villages' mushroomed on almost every continent, providing programmes of organised activities from jogging at dawn to late night discotheque parties so that visitors could remain hermetically sealed in, save for an occasional shopping or sightseeing foray. Theme parks like Walt Disney's in California and Florida, and cruise ships resembling floating resorts became destinations in themselves. The generation of packaged charter flight jetsetters accelerated into full swing. These were not individuals who made independent choices about their daily life on holiday but the completely processed, packaged brigade; they flew in, checked in, remained oblivious to their surroundings beyond being in another sunspot, and barely needed to change their money into local currency, let alone hear the native tongue. Against this all-inclusive formula, Switzerland's summer-market share dipped but the popular skiing boom happened concurrently, providing a new lucrative branch of tourism, even if its growth would eventually provide militant environmentalists with more anti-tourism ammunition. The pattern of Switzerland's tourism changed with visitor levels becoming almost equally divided between winter and summer. Now increasing numbers of destinations put on the map by the packaged holiday explosion – including many on the shores of the Mediterranean which sacrificed everything to exploit a greedy short-term dash for maximum growth – are on the decline, demolished by the monster of tourism they created. The concrete canyon high-rises and sprawling hedonistic development, which used to attract the budget holiday-maker seeking cheap sun, now repels as much as the polluted beaches and seas. The catch cry is: Can any paradise survive tourism?

In Switzerland's case the answer must be in the affirmative and the country is harvesting the fruits of having basically preserved those qualities which first tempted visitors in Victorian times landscape, fresh air, tranquillity and the opportunity for healthy sporting holidays. The summer holiday in the mountains is now enjoying a renaissance. The wheel has turned full circle, although under scrutiny; the upturn in fortunes is, fundamentally, the traditional Swiss product enjoying renewed demand because of the sea change from insufferably spoiled resorts to 'unspoilt' venues. Never mind if this resembles the travel business's equivalent of praising a woman for being fashionable because she has kept her miniskirt in the closet until short skirts came back 'in'!

Marco Solari, longtime head of Ticino tourism, is adamant that Switzerland should not sit back and wait for its turn in the cycle to come around. ' We are not a museum, Switzerland cannot be the museum of Europe. You can't build your fortune on the misfortune of others – it's very important. We are not strong because others are weak, we are stronger when others are strong.' The discussion in Swiss tourism – the future of which depends on the turning it takes at the current crossroads after reflecting on and re-evaluating the industry – revolves around a spider's web of issues. Some of these issues – such as damage to the environment and too many visitors concentrated in high season in a handful of saturated resorts – Switzerland has in common with any country receiving tourism. Others are uniquely Swiss.

Walter Leu explained his version of the challenge facing the industry: 'We are aware that being in the centre of Europe, and in the middle of the Common Market there will be a tremendous demand for the alpine region and we have to find a balance – sufficient demand to keep business going but not to exaggerate business so that Switzerland will be destroyed by its tourism. Somehow, step-by-step, we have to transform a tourist mentality of consumerism into a more responsible one... I believe that from now on destinations which do not succeed in protecting the environment will fade out of business. According to a news poll, 60 per cent of potential guests said that when making a decision about a holiday destination they looked at the environmental situation in a country first.'

The phenomenon of an enlightened, more green-aware visitor is appealing but Professor Krippendorf is just one of the many who has doubts about whether this idealistic species exists in any great numbers – a holiday-maker unselfishly prepared to compromise on his vacation aspirations in the cause of doing his bit to save the environment? He emphasises that tourists are escapists and they do not want reality to intrude into their leisure time for fear that the latter is impaired with the kind of problems daily life is plagued with – from which they are on holiday.

It seems to me that Switzerland would like its tourists to be mirror images of the Swiss themselves when they travel abroad – good spenders, courteous and well-behaved. Yet a barrage of critical charges can be levelled against the Swiss for their vacationing habits at home, which have not been entirely beyond reproach when it comes to apportioning blame for environmental abuse. Many seem to be worryingly content with being pseudo-environmentalists, only prepared to pay cosmetic service to environmental protection where it is not inconvenient and does not necessitate their making sacrifices in their own prosperous lifestyles, especially where secondary weekend and holiday homes in the mountains are concerned. These, militant greens stridently denounce on the basis that demand for them has spawned Saturn-like rings of under-utilised, energy-wasteful apartment blocks around popular resorts close to Geneva and Zurich. Villages have developed haphazardly into towns urbanised to the extent of parking meters, one-way systems and traffic jams, as the octopus of suburbia has swallowed up green, wide-open spaces in a country which is already densely populated.

Krippendorf is deliberately explicit on where the axe should fall – and why it is slow to do so: 'We should restrict construction zones to contain development so there's not expansion again and again. But we have liberty of ownership – it's a kind of holy cow and you cannot touch this private property notion. If we tackled this ecological conflict it would be very unpopular and we live in a democracy where getting a majority of people to accept things which are not in their short-term interest is a kind of insoluble problem.'

In addition, in Switzerland if voters do not agree, the central state cannot overrule communal and cantonal autonomy. This system, combining a conservative mentality with a stiff innate resistance to change, means that the business of policy-making is reactive rather than proactive. For example, the Swiss took restrictive measures to protect their flora and fauna only when the picking of wild flowers reached the extent that it threatened the very existence of the Edelweiss. But when they decide to be innovative they can be second to none. For tourists, Swissair's 'Fly-Rail' scheme, which enables passengers to check luggage straight through to their home airports from any of 100 train stations, is a triumph. It's a stroke of pure organisational genius – in which other country could you do that with the slightest expectation of ever seeing your suitcase again?

It is that high standard that everything is relative to. Many a Swiss lobbyist claims that although Switzerland seems to be in the first rank of nations in the environmental protection league, it does not actually tackle the really fundamental issues, while prospective tourists overseas hold the country up as a perfect prototype of impeccable cleanliness. Who can really blame those of us inured to big city life with its gridlocked traffic, fumes, uncollected garbage and deplorable quality of life?

I was absolutely astonished the first time I saw people swimming in the lake in Zurich one hot day, considering that many a European city is still struggling to clean up polluted rivers and lakes to a point where fish can live in them, let alone make them clean for the odd dip.

Switzerland has a number of trump cards in its hand to play when it comes to avoiding the pollution traps that more recent, poorer tourist industries have fallen into. It had an infrastructure which could absorb the additional demands tourism places on a host country's resources, unlike some countries which, in their haste to acquire the foreign revenue-earning asset of a tourism business, build hotel rooms before the necessary foundation of sewerage, water and other support facilities. Switzerland is also so small that respect for the environment is second nature because any damaging build-up is felt more quickly and intensely than in other larger countries whose sheer physical size can absorb a larger degree before they qualify as being harmfully polluted. It is not tourists qua tourists which threatens the ecology but too many of them, and Switzerland has never developed mass tourism on the scale of that on the Spanish coasts. In fact, militant greens campaign not against weight of numbers but rather the low occupancy rate of the hotelerie, chalets and apartments. They advocate a clampdown on building and argue for a swing back to hotels, a move which Krippendorf endorses:' Big hotels use much less ground than the same quantity of secondary homes, so from the landscape point of view the concentration of tourists in hotels is not only economical but ecologically much more interesting.'

Although Switzerland has avoided the catastrophic mistake of building the grotesquely ugly purpose-built ski stations that other nations have disfigured their mountains with in order to get on the map in the ski holiday market, the proliferation in only a few years of the elaborate infrastructure of cable cars, ski lifts and secondary transport facilities used by skiers for barely a quarter of the year has got to the stage where it is impinging on the summer tourism scene. The opposition is to the eyesore of redundant-in-summer ironmongery of ski lifts on grassy hiking slopes, the detrimental effect a season of skiing inflicts on the vegetation, and the shattering interruption to the silence and solitude by the perpetual building of another wave of skiing-related facilities during August.

The uneven distribution pattern of tourists, which sees some resorts saturated for just four peak months – with skiers in February and March, and summer holiday-makers in July and August – is another sphere of concern to the Swiss. 80 per cent of tourists from North America and the Far East focus on some ten of over 200 destinations in Switzerland (including Geneva, Interlaken, St. Moritz, Zermatt, Lucerne and Montreux). There is no instant palliative for it, although the SNTO hopes that by educating visitors they can spread the load more equitably both physically and financially. Pragmatists tend to dismiss this laudable objective as wishful thinking because it is a basic fact of international travel that tourists who fly half-way around the world tend to insist on heading for famous sights that they can boast to their friends about when they get home, not remote places of which no one has ever heard, however worth visiting they might be. The experience of every popular tourist destination – from an overflowing St. Mark's Square in Venice to a packed Westminster Abbey in London – underlines the persistent failure to persuade peak-period crowds to visit in the quieter off-season, or to deflect them away to more obscure attractions. Another

theoretical suggestion to help ease the congestion is to stagger school holidays, although, again, this seems more of an academic discussion rather than a move any government is going to be bold enough to implement. And at least two of the mainstream Swiss top spots regard their swarms of visitors as tangible evidence of marketing success and a good reason to celebrate, which would turn to concern if the numbers dwindled.

To me Montreux and Lucerne stand out as shining examples of Swiss stereotypes with not a lot more going for them than simply being nice Swiss towns on pleasant lakes. Both depend heavily on tourism; they recognised that standing still signalled death, trained binoculars on the future, conceived new roles for themselves, and went out and sold them. Montreux now has half the number of beds it had before World War I and you can gauge the span between tourism then and now by crossing the road from the handsome facade of the Palace Hotel – a bastion of the Belle Epoque – to the hi-tech, cavernous, steel-and-glass emporium which is the fountain of its present prosperity. Yesteryear's wealthy replaced by today's big spender – the multinational corporate executive flying between continents with an unlimited expense account. The money-spinning conference business has seen the town's 1973 convention centre double in size, first in 1981, and then again in the '90s. The money-no-object criterion of the lifestyles of vice presidents and sales managers means that Montreux needs two of the regular type of tourist to equal the expenditure of a single convention guest. The once classy air of the promenade has given way to a more urban strip feel and the retired British who used to constitute a sizeable proportion of the visitors have been replaced by a younger clientele flocking to the annual Golden Rose TV competition and the jazz festival, which are pillars of the town's second lease of life. It is telling that the art galleries now exhibit bold abstracts of saxophonists alongside the touristy oils of one of Switzerland's best-known sights – the nearby Castle of Chillon.

Lucerne has also waged a progressive and aggressive marketing campaign to woo visitors under the leadership of the dynamic director of tourism, Kurt Illi. He comes from a corporate marketing background and brings to the tourism milieu a different, more professional outlook than those hampered by a local perspective shaped solely by the preservationist mentality of the isolated mountain communities. He is not averse to the odd gimmick, which has earned him some detractors among the old guard, and what he preaches particularly convincingly against is complacency, because it leads to stagnation. 'Too many people think that the landscape, mountains, snow and lakes are enough – that we can live on that for another 30 years. Switzerland has the perfect ground material but we have to add 20 or 30 per cent new ideas to mix with our natural products.' He focused Lucerne's drive for new markets on the Far East – Hong Kong, Korea, Singapore, and Japan – and berates fellow Swiss who 'blinkeredly' saw only Japan as the new market, 'and headed there stopping in Hong Kong only for duty free shopping.' The dividends for Lucerne are that Illi's policy has broken the town's over-dependence on the American market – a hangover in popularity from the GI days – to the extent that a quarter of its visitors now are from Asia, including a large number of Japanese who come to get married in a lakeside chapel. He is the dynamic face of Swiss tourism prepared to cut through bureaucracy and red tape in a system so organised to favour the bigger, more successful resorts. Unlike the tourism industry in neighbouring Austria, Germany and France, where the tourist offices are part of the political administration, Swiss tourism at a local level is privatised.

This discriminates against the minor resorts which simply cannot summon up the resources to develop, promote and market themselves. Inevitably rationalisation results, and the gap between an A-team of 'super resorts' and the others widens. The vicious circle of another layer of overcrowding in the major ones – like high ski resorts assuring snow by altitude and artificial snow guns, or the universally well-known summer success stories like Zermatt – is fueled. 'That's competition – survival of the fittest,' commented Gottfried Künzi of the Swiss Tourist Federation unapologetically, when I queried the wisdom of this approach.

As fundamental to the future as the question of which resorts remain financially viable is whether today's Swiss, with one of the highest standards of living in Europe, actively wish to remain in the tourist game or feel the price to the environment and the indigenous population is too high. There are plenty of indications that patience with the downside of tourism is wearing thin, especially in destinations where, in high season, the locals feel they are virtually living in tourist-occupied territory. It is the younger generation which seems to be contracting the virus of 'hospitality fatigue' with a more sceptical approach to the necessity of tourism than their fathers and grandfathers had in whose lives it played an even more important economic role. Switzerland's dilemma is whether it is viable to run an environmentally compatible tourism industry. Krippendorf's route toward equalising the scales is the theory of 'soft tourism'. 'This is something like a magic square with four corners: economic profitability, satisfaction of the tourists, equilibrium and culture of the indigenous people, the quality of the countryside and nature...' In the past, priority has been focused largely on short-term economic profitability with satisfaction of the tourist coming second at the expense of the other two.

In fact, Switzerland, whose charted course through the ocean of tourism has been one of quality rather than quantity, is well suited for 'soft tourism'. It is simply too tiny for mass tourism – to the evident relief of both visitor and host. The backbone of the hotel structure remains old-style, often family-run establishments which cannot accommodate the numbers of holiday-makers who invade parts of the Mediterranean coast and islands. In 1990, 75 per cent of Switzerland's 6,700 hotels had 25 rooms or less and 44 per cent had fewer than ten. If Switzerland is to welcome larger numbers – and there are predictions of an increase to 100 million overnights by the end of the century – it desperately wants quality, big-spending visitors like business incentive groups and more well-heeled holiday-makers but not the large turnover/small profit margin of the charter flight packaged client, for whom it is too expensive anyway.

Among the other relevant factors affecting the future of the tourism scene is the level of ill will in Swiss public opinion. Whether immigrant workers or overseas tourists, there seems an inclination to bracket them together as a commodity which is needed economically, tolerated, but not necessarily welcomed or liked. It ought to sound alarm bells that this attitude showed up in a survey whose findings indicated that the Swiss are regarded by visitors as being unfriendly towards tourists. Neither do the Swiss like working in the hotel business – and so they don't. Today 'Swiss service' is more likely to mean Yugoslav, Portuguese or Sri Lankan and many acknowledge the problem as being one peculiar to tourism in a wealthy society. With the employment choices that a highly developed country offers, the Swiss favour white-collar jobs instead of the often dirty work and unsocial hours involved in the hotel and catering trade.

The state of the tourism discussion reflects Switzerland's own identity crisis. It has had a privileged run touristically speaking – thanks to an early start and special advantages like its neutrality lending it the priceless drawcard of a safe-holiday-haven image and the gift of the Alps – but is in danger of suffering from a hint of complacency. Just as it was not difficult to be the world's premier banking haven when there was only one, these days 'the gnomes of Zurich' find themselves to be just another financial centre among many. It is a new world, and a tougher one for the Swiss now that, as the Foreign Minister put it recently, they have become 'a normal country like any other.'

But as a tourism veteran Switzerland is staying competitively in training, with statistics of the opening years of the nineties showing them to be among the best ever, while some sprinting competitors are falling behind, burnt out – mainly from 'injuries' like environmental pollution. Tourism ranks as the largest and fastest growing industry in the world and Switzerland's future as the leading alpine playground of Europe must have an optimistic future – particularly, if this writer could presumptuously suggest, if the leading lights in the tourism business borrow just a touch of that highly admirable entrepreneurial magic the Swiss watch industry utilised when it fought back with Swatch.

Tradition and Modernity in Switzerland
Pietro Bellasi

1. The Swiss Paradox

The 'Swiss road to modernity', and to the cosmopolitanism inherent in it, is marked by continual, tireless, almost manic efforts to preserve and revitalise local traditions. That locally-oriented traditionalism is in fact the key to any understanding of the Swiss form of modernity and is one of the many contradictions that characterise the country.

It is, for example, paradoxical that Switzerland should be wealthy despite the 'poor' soil and the dramatically furrowed terrain that makes it a small, stormy sea of rocks and crags. Affluent despite the total absence of raw materials, or the difficulties of communication that may exist even between two neighbouring villages, separated perhaps by immense, jagged masses of granite. Paradoxical, too, the essential unity which can integrate diverse, in some ways antithetical ethnic groups, cultures, languages and religions.

It is important to emphasise that the paradox of close, efficient links between modernity and tradition remains viable only because of a common goal shared by both the processes of modernisation and the national commitment to preserve and reactivate traditions. That goal is the thorough, all-pervasive aestheticisation of everyday life, in other words what Bernard Crettaz, curator of European Ethnography at the Musée d'Ethnographie of Geneva, terms *joli*. What he means is that apart from watches, pharmaceuticals, chocolate and powdered milk, Switzerland also specialises in the manufacture of products that are 'pretty' or 'charming'. *La production du joli* may indeed, according to Crettaz, be one of the fundamental and characteristic elements of the collective Swiss self-image – the culture of 'Swissness'.

Another expert in collective self-images and everyday life, the French anthropologist Georges Auclair, maintains that modernity consists in the simultaneous coexistence of two different 'conceptual worlds' which, far from cancelling one another out, are indissolubly intertwined and complementary. He calls them the 'twofold conceptual worlds of modernity'. The most advanced contemporary societies, as Auclair sees it, produce two distinct sets of collective self-images which act as a mirror for themselves and others. The French anthropologist calls one of these systems the 'Faustian conceptual world': the Promethean faith in progress, particularly in science and technology; the collective enthusiasm for space exploration, computers, electronic gadgetry and the omnipresence of the mass-media.

He identifies the other system as the 'Franciscan conceptual world': the production of nostalgia and revivals of the past, but also the 'ecological' pangs of conscience in the face of nature defiled, brutalised and enslaved, and the fear that nature may take its revenge in the form of biblical disasters or mysterious, insidious plagues. It also includes a longing for the 'natural', 'authentic', 'original' and 'unspoilt'; an infatuation with the exotic and the esoteric, with astrology, fortune-telling and magic in general; and the boom in macrobiotics, the mystique of the body, and alternative therapies (so-called 'soft medicine'). But it consists above all in an agitated, feverish, occasionally anxiety-ridden discovery and revitalisation of traditions, regionalisms and localisms which run counter to (but must coexist with) cosmopolitanism and the uprootedness of the 'global village'. The most interesting aspect of Auclair's thesis is that although mutually incompatible these two mentalities, these two ways of experiencing the adventure of modernity, do not preclude or neutralise each other. Not only do they coexist, they even seem to provide mutual impulses, to encourage and invigorate one another. In other words, the production of nostalgia is as essential for the development of modern society and the modern mentality as the manufacture of computers and robotic equipment.

It might be useful at this point to refer to the results of a recent survey conducted in northern Italy on the mentality of executives in large industrial concerns: when faced with negotiations or important decisions, many of them first explored all the rational strategies, tactics and calculations, and if these failed, abandoned their armies of technical experts and resorted to – let us say – para-magical means, for example the services of a fortune-teller. And, this phenomenon appears to be much more widespread in the industrialised world than generally imagined.

I am convinced that few countries in the world push the functional interdependency between the 'Faustian' or 'Promethean' and 'Franciscan' or 'traditional naturalist' conceptual worlds to such extremes. The point where the two apparently irreconcilable cultural and intellectual trends meet is in the aestheticisation of everyday life.

2. Let's Take the Train!

To shed more light on this latter concept, we can turn to the simple 'metaphors', or 'symptoms' as it were, of everyday life and look at some examples. As our first typically Swiss metaphor, let's take the train, the technological object par excellence, a symbol of what might be defined as 'beneficent technology'. Responsible for ending the isolation between valleys and ethnic groups, and between Switzerland and the rest of Europe, the Swiss train has become the protagonist of a virtual modern myth. I think it is only in Switzerland (particularly in certain French- and German-speaking cantons) that a bookshop window could be devoted wholly, or at least partly, to literature and picture-books dealing specifically with the federal railway system, books describing its daring routes, powerful old locomotives and speedy, glossy, modern trains – with the occasional nod to 'trains of other lands'. *The Last Swiss Steam Locomotives, The Electric Locomotives of the Federal Railways between the Wars, Private Swiss Railways, The St Gotthard Line and its History, The Glacier Express:* in these titles, general history is filtered through railway history and seems to follow the rhythms of a highly punctual railway timetable. In many photographic calendars – the true clinical test of our monomanias and neuroses – dogs, cats, alpine flowers and exotic birds often cede pride of place to pictures of trains old and new; or to landscapes in which the train speeding past is presented as an innocuous, integral part of a natural landscape: a mere breeze brushing by waterfalls, flowering trees, lakes and vineyards. Another considerable element of this modern myth and the little everyday rituals that go hand in hand with it is the world of model trains – the passion for collecting and playing with miniature trains that travel through more or less complex reconstructions of landscapes. As Claude Lévi-Strauss, one of the pioneers of contemporary anthropology, shows in *La pensée sauvage,* the 'miniature model' has at all times and in all cultures been a fundamental anthropological pattern: the means by which reality – complex, often ambiguous, occasionally frightening and threatening – can be symbolically summed up at a glance and controlled by a single hand. The model is elevated to a sacred icon, the 'fetish' of a situation that is both exemplary and problematic. For Lévi-Strauss the 'miniature model' is even the source of the aesthetic enjoyment of works of art, as a symbolic means of controlling reality. No matter how gigantic or monumental (Lévi-Strauss cites the Sistine Chapel as an example), the work of art is always created by 'subtraction', by reducing infinitely differentiated reality to the 'simplified' fixity of symbolic representation. Thus, even the Sistine Chapel, both monumental fresco and affirmation of the Roman Catholic empire, becomes an immediately comprehensible synthesis of the complex Counter-Reformation cosmogony. If we turn our attention to 'other' civilisations, many pre-industrial peoples would construct a 'miniature model', a sort of 'sculpture' of the village, beside the hut of the witch-doctor or chief: it was the village of the dead and a means of claiming possession of the territory of the living.

But let us return to our model trains. A nationwide survey carried out by Swiss Italian Radio revealed that there are more model train collectors in Switzerland than anywhere else in Europe. A number of watch factories have even been converted to the production of 'super models' – miniature trains so accurate that they resemble 'real' trains down to the tiniest details. A model train can easily cost more than 50,000 Swiss francs.

We shall return to the subject of miniaturisation later, for it is basic to an understanding of certain aspects of the aestheticisation of everyday life in Switzerland. For the moment it is enough to point out that miniaturisation has become a ritualistic, iconographic support for a technological myth. The scale model also represents the origins of aesthetic enjoyment: it allows us to grasp, control and 'colonise' an object, rendering it not only unique and precious but symbolically charged and powerful as well.

We should add that in Switzerland the 'real' train (the one on a scale of 1:1) is both an extremely advanced technological system (one of the most modern in the world) and a fundamental element in the aestheticisation of everyday life. We have already described the richness of the applicable iconography: in no other country do we find such a strong commitment to including the train as an integral element of the natural landscape, of its beauty and cleanliness. This is one of the many effects of the *joli* or *enjolivement* (prettification) mentioned by Bernard Crettaz, and demonstrated by tourist guides, photographic calendars, publicity brochures, the little pictures fixed to the walls of train compartments, even on stamps. The brilliance of the eternal snow and glaciers contrasts with the tiny cog-railway trains, impeccably enamelled in fiery red; gigantic fir forests and massive grey outcrops of granite swallow and disgorge long, thin, green and silver worms of fast Intercity trains.

The advertising and customer services could not be more 'advanced' or pleasant either. Every station, however, large or small, has the long magazine racks with dozens of brochures extolling the wonders of what might be called the 'great game' or 'great hobby' of train travel. So much so that the dozens of available group excursions include 'surprise tours', destination unknown. Then there are the 'kindergarten carriages': 'Away with boredom! In the new family carriages, the children have a playroom all to themselves, with toy telephones, slides, swings, safe soft floors, and a range of children's books (2–7 years and 7–12 years). The carriage also has a nappy-changing room, a space for push-chairs and tables for older children to play at. It's easy to find the family carriages: they are in the second class section, and are marked on the outside with a big friendly bear.' 'Get on a bike at the station' – invites another brochure, and offers a basic model (with six gears), a children's model or a mountain bike (with 18 gears). There is also a booklet containing 40 suggested trips, with full colour pictures.

Then there is the *silentium wagen*, which I have never managed to travel in. Presumably it is designed for secretaries with their portable computers, accountants, journalists, misanthropic writers, hermits, monks and neurasthenics on holiday.

In any case, the interiors of the carriages, the asceticism of their essential furnishings, verging on the austere and clinical, are among those privileged places where design is not as important as another typically Swiss quality: the calligraphy of cleanliness, a corollary of the production of the pretty and quaint. (What this involuntarily calls to mind is the 'helvetica' type face adopted by many railway and underground train networks throughout the world because of its immediate clarity.) Even the materials used in the carriages represent an attempt to achieve a sort of bare, absolute tidiness; an anaesthetic, puritanical honesty reminiscent of the hygienic, sanitary functionalism of the dental surgery, and totally free of any form of wickedly aesthetic claims. If there is an aesthetic at all, it is one of refinement. One could even imagine these materials to have been assembled here for the sole purpose of providing the trains, inside and out, with a gloss of 'finish' (real or purported). Aluminium and steel, satinised to give them the sheen of precious metals; generously proportioned fittings on a pitiless continuity of blank surfaces; screws with perfectly oriented crosses; plastic components set here and there like gemstones; net curtains, which reveal the passing landscape as through a pair of sunglasses; retractable tables and rubbish bins which close with a sharp click, coming to rest softly and silently against little rubber cushions.

3. A Culture of Finish and Maintenance
It is in Switzerland's trains that one begins to understand that – be it architecture, road-signs, parks, city pavements, bridges, public lavatories, shop signs or any other facet of the townscape, even in high tension pylons and manholes – finish is not simply an extra, a kind of lavish prodigality invested in the superficial structure of everyday objects. In Switzerland the finish is in itself a structure; that is to say, a cultural structure, a vehicle of the technological aestheticisation of everyday life. To spin the thread a bit further, we might say that the culture of everyday Swiss life is a culture of finish and its corollary, maintenance. Both methods of aestheticising the environment and everyday objects seem to create a site at the very heart of everyday life where technological innovation and the tradition of craftsmanship are reconciled. Though this is not the place for it, I am convinced that an anthropological analysis of the concept and practice of maintenance could reveal many interesting aspects of the

mentality and everyday culture of Switzerland. Practised with enthusiasm and persistence throughout the country, maintenance is primarily an almost manic battle against the signs, traces and symptoms of decline and decay. Hence, it is essentially a battle against the signs, or rather the open wounds, of the passing of time; against transience and mortality. Thus maintenance goes hand in hand with the legendary Swiss cleanliness whose genesis, history and characteristics were so well analysed and illustrated some years ago in Geneviève Heller's book *Propre en ordre*.

It is well-known that from an anthropological point of view death is perceived as decay, corruption and putrefaction; in essence as dirt. Cleanliness (and order) are therefore in some way a means of warding off death and its disorderly, retrogressive degeneration. In the final analysis, might we not see the extraordinary commitment to the pursuit of cleanliness and maintenance as a symptom of the profound unease the idea of death creates in the collective imagination? Swept out the door along with the great tragedies of history, death comes back in through the window in the form of an oppressive, monotonous everyday life that is perceived as 'compulsive repetitiveness'.

We have thus far interpreted the propensity for 'finish' as a symptom of the aestheticisation of everyday life that is pursued with such untiring commitment. The effort involved is evident, but to my mind it conceals a further latent motive already noted at the beginning of this essay: the fretful, sometimes anguished quest for an at least somewhat plausible reconciliation between technical and cosmopolitan modernity and the local, personalised, craftsmanly tradition responsible for 'quality of life'.

4. Let's Look at Our Watches!

It is interesting to note that this very quest has formed the nucleus, or dramatic countercurrents, of the recent history of that most archetypal of Swiss products: the watch.

Visitors to such watch-making regions as the Jura around La Chaux-de-Fonds or Le Locle will immediately be struck by a surprising contrast or contradiction: they will note that the top floor of some of the farm houses in the hills or the countryside – the ones whose roofs slope down to the level of the grass – has a kind of long bow window, a continuous row of windows that jut out beyond the façade. This used to be the watch-maker's workshop, which many farming and herding families installed in their homes; it was used chiefly on long, freezing winter days.

The link between the farming tradition and watch-making is also visible in another curious and apparently secondary detail: some Swiss museums (particularly the museum in Neuchâtel) contain collections of wonderful scale models – there is miniaturisation again! – astonishing miniatures of the objects and tools of everyday rural life, for example carts and carriages of all shapes and sizes. Their execution, in wood with metal fittings, is absolutely extraordinary, particularly for the care taken with the tiniest details: for example, the nails, which fix the iron rims to wooden wheels that often measure only two or three centimetres in diameter. The perfection of these tiny details immediately indicates that these little masterpieces were the work of watch-makers; the subjects represented also show that they were designed and constructed by watch-makers/farmers either during their leisure hours or when work was scarce.

Leaving the valleys and mountains for La Chaux-de-Fonds, one is brutally confronted with the 'other' aspect of this typically Swiss activity. Though it is a small town, or perhaps a large village, there is nothing 'joli' about this capital of chronometry – what it lacks is precisely the prettiness that belongs to the cultural baggage of even Switzerland's large conurbations. With its network of perpendicular streets, the total absence of an 'historical centre', and even a certain amount of disorderly architectural squalor and untamed chaos, it looks like a little grey blemish, an alien element in the idyllic dream of the green Swiss countryside and the black forests of the Jura; a scab, a little concrete aberration in the very heart of the luxuriant verdure of Switzerland. La Chaux-de-Fonds has always been the symptom of a radical contradiction that not even the Swiss myth of harmony and order, with all its rituals, has managed to heal: 'We often imagine the little watch-making town to be 'clean and orderly'. Not a bit of it. Like other industrial cities, La Chaux-de-Fonds developed in a climate of anarchy and moral disorder. From 1850, for a number of decades, it resembled a town in a western film, with its centres of corruption, a continuous turnover of population, a degree of ferment that wearies the imagination today.' These are the words of Jean-Marc Barrelet, the historian of the watch-making industry, in *Life in the Watch-making Towns in the 19th century: From the Craftsman's Bench to the Machine* an article published in the anthology *Everyday Life in Switzerland since 1300*. Barrelet goes on to write: 'In the 19th century, La Chaux-de-Fonds and the watch-making towns of the Jura were not spared the problems that all industrial towns face today: Christianity's loss of credibility, dissolute morals, the influx of all manner of homeless people in search of work. In the middle of the century the town saw its population grow by almost 23,000. This mini-migration to the west brought with it vagabonds, adulterated alcohol, cabarets and brothels: a heterogeneous society whose morals were out of step with the tastes of the puritanical, God-fearing local worthies. There was a gulf between the demands of morality and the needs of urban development, between austerity and prosperity. A close observer of life in La Chaux-de-Fonds, Charles-Eugène Tissot, opposed the opening of café music-halls: 'This evening we have seen the Havert Inn transformed into a music-hall. Madame Mercier sang some patriotic airs and a large number of somewhat risqué ballads passably well. The artist's dress was more than immodest: décolleté to the waist, arms bare to the shoulders... I for one do not appreciate this French style of dressing, for its influence on public morality can only be a negative one.'

The watch is thus a tangible symbol, a mythical object – perhaps even a fetish – which seems to contain within its precious, sealed case the secret of reconciling the opposed, dynamic elements of rustic, rural tradition and the innovative modernity of precision mechanics and micro-electronics. After all, the watch is an 'instrument' that transforms the linear time of history and scientific and technological 'progress' into the cyclical time of everyday life. However slow it is, every wheel mechanism ultimately returns to its point of origin. The 'circular' logic of the watch mechanism suggests the intellectual myth of eternal recurrence and the mechanical myth of perpetual motion. 'Switzerland is a country that lives in rhythms and cadences, while linear, goal-directed time is relegated totally to the sphere of the major industries, which work far away, beyond the horizons of everyday life.' Thus spoke Fabrizio Sabelli, professor of Economic Anthropology at the University of Neuchâtel, in a recent interview. 'A feat of craftsmanship, an artefact, like a watch creating time, is there to demonstrate that real historical time is entirely relative in importance.' And Sabelli adds: 'The obsession of everyday life in Switzerland, fixated as it is on rhythms and exact cadences, is nothing less than a highly intelligent, highly efficient way of stopping time and imprisoning it in the present and the commonplace. Chronographic time, with its rhythmic pattern and infinite divisions, is time that has been stopped, arrested like the arrow in Zeno's paradox. But even more than this, it is formal time, mechanical time; its contents cannot be anything but everyday life and its ritualised repetitions. History is banished from this all-pervasive present. The innermost preoccupation of the average Swiss is remaining true to present temporality, a temporality that is rigidly structured and painstakingly rhythmic. All of this has profound and unexpected consequences: the Swiss present dramatically, sometimes tragically, dominates and overshadows the country's intellectual, cultural, philosophical and even political scene. I believe that the refusal on the part of so many intellectuals, but also of 'ordinary' people, to take part in the celebrations of Switzerland's 700-year-anniversary should be interpreted less as political and ideological opposition or sheer indifference than as fear, a sense of anxiety in the face of the risk of acquiring a purely historical identity, which the Swiss would perceive as a shirt of Nessus – poisoned with a disturbing otherness. Rhythmical patterns are also a condition for that everyday efficiency – in the service sector, for example – for which the Confederation is legendary. 'The Swatch,' Sabelli concludes, 'has catapulted the Swiss watchmaking industry into the most advanced modernity thanks to its marketing philosophy (the watch as a fashion item to be changed regularly), manufacturing technology, design, marketing and distribution networks, etc. But the Swatch is above all the symbol of a quasi-mythical tradition compatible with the immediate present, and in fact penetrating powerfully to its very heart. It would actually be time to change the Swiss flag: a Swatch should replace the white cross. The identity of the hour, the minute and the second – the identity of the rhythm of everyday life — should replace the historical identity invoked by the cross.'

It should also be added that the watch itself and the way it is produced (a maximum of work with a minimum of material) once again represent the dynamics of the miniaturisation already noted above. Jean-Marc Barrelet has told me that the highest aspiration and ambition, the supreme dream, of every watch-maker is to enclose the most complicated, sophisticated mechanism in the smallest possible case. Is there a need to stress the extent to which the watch is synonymous with finish and maintenance?

The watch might therefore be described as a symbol of a successful synthesis: the reconciliation of tradition and modernity, one of the fundamental elements of cultural tension in the Swiss mentality and way of life, of what might be termed 'the Swiss conceptual world'. Characteristically enough, reconciliation occurs yet again as the aestheticisation of a perpetually reaffirmed everyday life, the punctilious miniaturised exactitude of whose rhythms and immutable cadences run counter to the linear dynamic of the march of history – the latter often perceived by Swiss public opinion as 'the others' madness'. To stay at the level of metaphor and 'cultural symptoms', with regard to both the intentions of its inhabitants and administrators and in practice, the 'industrial village' of La Chaux-de-Fonds is simply an extreme case, in the Swiss context, of that same tension and same attempts at reconciliation. For decades the touristic slogan of the watch-making capital has been: 'La Chaux-de-Fonds, the town that wants to live in the country.' Jean-Marc Barrelet, in an interview on Swiss Italian Radio, stressed yet again: 'La Chaux-de-Fonds first saw the light of day as an industrial town in the 19th century. Originally a pastoral community, from around 1850, it became an industrial community, while jealously preserving its rural roots and a certain agricultural air in the midst of its urban context: though set in the middle of the countryside, it is entirely dependent on industry. In fact, the rural nature of La Chaux-de-Fonds is entirely mythical. The town depends on its industry, and an extremely vulnerable industry at that; an economic crisis would be capable of jeopardising the town's survival. This situation is unique in Switzerland. Berne will never disappear, nor will Geneva or Zurich, barring some terrible disaster. But when the watch-making industry was going through its great crisis in the 1970s, it was easy to imagine closing down La Chaux-de-Fonds and throwing away the keys. On the other hand, the Council of Europe chose La Chaux-de-Fonds in order to study this interesting aspect from a cultural perspective: it may be characteristic that the town had a theatre before it had a hospital. Obviously, apart from maintaining a tradition, watch-making attracts culture; there can be no watch-making industry without a major art school. It was not by chance that Le Corbusier came from La Chaux-de-Fonds, where he attended just such a school. It is a town which had an art museum very early on, because in order to make beautiful things you have to have beauty close at hand. Apart from the fact that watch-makers always travelled far and wide to bring back new ideas from their travels.'

5. The Industry of 'Prettiness' and Death

In 1991, Zurich's Museum of Applied Arts organised an exhibition of Swiss poster art, considered among the best in the world. Among the many exhibits was one long used worldwide by the Swiss tourist industry: it shows a little lamb with a flower in its mouth, gambolling in a miniature landscape (!) of mountains, pastures, hills and quaint old villages. Even in more recent tourist posters there is not a trace of motorways, modern buildings, harried crowds or bustling technological and post-modern activity – except, as already noted, for trains, funicular railways, cable-cars and romantic steamboats, represented as elements of a kind of 'secondary nature'. But the protagonists on the posters are still lakes, waterfalls, valleys, chalets and mountains: pre-industrial landscapes, half-deserted, echoing or silent. The post-modern Switzerland of powerful multinationals, the Switzerland of a highly advanced service-industry providing jobs for 60 per cent of the workforce, the Switzerland of the megalopolis which incorporates villages and cities in an agglomerative continuum from Romanshorn to Geneva is as assiduously avoided as the real Switzerland that has 450 automobiles for every 1,000 inhabitants. The real Switzerland, whose 'ancient villages' close down at the end of the summer or winter holidays like fairgrounds, is nowhere to be found.

The images and practices of the tourist industry (both at home and abroad) are another outstanding example of the way the collective image of 'everyday culture' in Switzerland deals with the relationship between modernisation and tradition. Here, however, 'the touristic metaphor' reveals an aspect undisclosed by our analysis thus far. The reconciliation between modernity and tradition often takes the form of concealment or, if we prefer, repression of all the elements, dynamics, problems, imbalances and 'disorders' of modern life. They make way for a simpler setting: the recreation or simulation of the 'genuine', 'unspoilt' world of pastoral, alpine rusticity. This decontextualisation leads to a kind of 'detemporalisation': to a kind of absolute present, an eternal ordinariness that superimposes itself on a nostalgic reconstruction of the past. This process often assumes feverish, compulsive forms. And this – not surprisingly – takes us back to our observations about the world of watches and their manufacture.

In the first scene of *The Triptych*, one of the last plays by the recently deceased Swiss author Max Frisch, the old protagonist talks to the ghosts of his dead relations. In response to his question of what 'eternity' might be, one of the spirits answers that 'eternity is simply banal'. Might the eternity to which Max Frisch alludes by any chance be the eternity of everyday life in his country? An everyday life based on simulation, and thus often hypocritical, moralistic, stagnant, dedicated to the preservation of the obvious and the quest for a sterile, paralysing idea of 'harmony'?

The same harmony which, from childhood onwards, shaped the suffering of another Swiss writer, Fritz Zorn. In his posthumously published book *Mars*, he wrote: 'The harmony of the world I grew up in was so perfect that it would have frightened off the most harmonious creature on earth. The Hamlet-like question looming over my home was: harmony, or not to be?' The harmony of Zorn's unhappy Switzerland also consisted of tranquillity, silence and, above all, of everyday peace and quiet: '... my concept of bourgeois existence strikes me as ultimately including something negative and evil, when it threatens to become identified with peace and quiet, that peace and quiet in turn being linked with everything that is clean, sterile, proper and comme il faut ...' The words 'peace and quiet' take on a sinister, horrifying air. In Switzerland everything must always be absolutely peaceful, and this need for tranquillity is expressed in the imperative. They issue the command: Quiet! as if decreeing: Death! Fritz Zorn understood the fatal tumour that had established itself and spread through his body as 'finally something unharmonious', something contradictory and antagonistic; something not 'propre en ordre', as Geneviève Heller would say, not 'sweet and pretty' to speak with Bernard Crettaz.

6. The Aestheticisation of Everyday Life

But let us return to the symptom of tourism, a particularly good place to encounter the aestheticisation of everyday life. At the conceptual level it appears as a repression of the processes of modernisation and experience of modern life and cosmopolitan chaos achieved through a rapturously nostalgic revival of an alpine idyll. At the level of real life, aestheticisation creates a harmonious bridge between the poles of tradition and modernity, one of the basic tensions affecting many aspects of everyday Swiss culture.

As I have already mentioned, Bernard Crettaz is curator of European Ethnography at Geneva's Museum of Ethnography, and has written a great deal about Switzerland. In the anthology *Everyday Life in Switzerland since 1300*, for example, he published an anthropological and semiological analysis of the great 'National Exhibitions', which he sees as an 'Identikit', a reflection of the self-image Switzerland has gradually created. I went to visit Crettaz in the village of his birth, Zinal, almost 2,000 metres above sea level. It is located in the Anniviers Valley in the Valais, a crevasse of granite and grass opening onto the Rhône Valley near the town of Sierre. For the same anthology, Bernard Crettaz and Yvonne Preiswerk collaborated on an article about the emblematic development of foreign and indigenous tourism in 'his' valley, *Tourism and everyday life 1900–1990 – the example of Zinal (Valais)*. I wanted to interview Crettaz for Radio Lugano. As my car climbed towards Zinal I realized how much the Anniviers Valley was a museum, a kind of open-air exhibition of the deeds and misdeeds of the tourist industry (catering in this case to foreign tourists in particular). Apart from what Crettaz calls the 'over-equipment' of the Alps (hotels, asphalted roads, nightclubs, boutiques, discos, swimming pools, tennis courts, shopping centres, folklore festivals, competitions, entertainment), what immediately strikes the eye are the 'holiday homes', with their vivid picture-postcard colours and improbably red geraniums.

Almost entirely eclipsed by them stand the few ancient or old houses (unrenovated) and the few *mazots* (traditional wooden constructions built on piles) with their split and dusty tree-trunks. Many of the new and restored houses have achieved an air reminiscent of the disturbing image of 'the dear departed', made up American style. They seem to have been on the receiving end of a tornado that has just come from a flea-market, and to have been buried under all the objects on sale. An assemblage of incongruous things, whose sole common denominator is the consuming nostalgia for a past whose scant relics they have collected with wistful pride: cartwheels (by the hundred), scales, copper pots, the improbable antlers of unspecified animals, keys, wall-clocks, battalions of garden gnomes, ox-yokes, milking stools, anthropomorphic roots, tree-trunks – and dozens of Swiss and Valais flags. I can still remember how, after seeing multitudes of tourists exhausted from the pursuit of relaxation and leisure, I finally came across two robust farmers, their clothes half torn. Feet planted firmly on an extremely steep slope, they were skilfully, imperturbably mowing hay amongst the legs of grazing cows. Crettaz greeted them with a wave and, in response to my enthusiasm, informed me with barely concealed irony verging on cynicism, that one was the manager and the other the assistant manager of a bank in a nearby town, intent on their favourite hobby: breeding cattle.

'Since 1700, we Swiss have owed the recognition of one of our specific qualitites to the tourist industry. The discovery of the mountains (an inestimable, national treasure) and the fact that in the 18th century the European bourgeoisie began travelling to Switzerland as tourists in ever larger numbers made us think we had discovered our own identity. The extraordinary link between tourism and our national identity can essentially be traced back to that era, when the country was trying to establish that its 'Swissness' derived from values which could serve as solid, durable points of reference for its specific national features. These values, represented above all by the Zurich School, but also by Jean-Jacques Rousseau and his French followers, suggested that the discovery of Switzerland was a further element in the discovery of nature, which in turn derived from the discovery of the mountains. In other words, the Swiss national identity was born at the very moment Switzerland became a tourist paradise. This is the crucial factor in the specific destiny of our country.'

'But,' Bernard Crettaz continues, 'the decisive revolution certainly came later, at the turn of the 20th century. I would call it the revolution of 'looking and being looked at'. The indigenous mountain population realised that 'the people from down below', the tourists from the cities, the valley towns and the plains, were looking at them; and in consequence, they began looking at themselves. It was when they perceived the relationship between observing and being observed that their own, unique identity was revealed to them. That is, through the curious gaze of the tourists they gained a fuller awareness of their own society, history, cultural heritage, landscape, rituals and even objects of daily use. Tourism has therefore been a powerful moving force in the revelation of local, regional and cantonal identity.

But it should also be added that when tourism arrived in the countryside and the mountains, it was the expression of a society that had resolved to dominate the old rural world. This gives rise to quite a surprising paradox: tourism brings with it – along with the other elements of modernity – urbanisation. And it is precisely at this point that the 'indigenous' people become aware of their material and cultural heritage. But what did this heritage consist of? Remnants, the last traces of the old mountain society. From here on the tourists' demands were fulfilled by an 'alpine supply'. The mountain people understood that they had to offer the tourists what they were looking for: the residues of their old crumbling culture. At this point they began to show them beautiful cottages, beautiful mazots in old villages, old tools and other utilitarian objects, and beautiful landscapes.

It was not until the post-war period and even into the '60s, in fact, that new tourist revolution set in, bringing the pressures of modernisation so strongly to bear that the old world of farmers and herdsmen literally exploded. During those years the very face of the countryside, the valleys and the mountains, underwent a twofold change. On the one hand there was a process of technological ultra-modernisation of the 'primitive' environment: a radical urbanisation involving the construction of a large number of new roads, motorways, ski lifts, hotels and resorts. But another, almost contradictory tendency also emerged: the 'old', the 'antique', the 'typical' – in short, simulated 'tradition' – began to be manufactured.

Nowadays, these trends are both extremely active. The tourist industry requires technological modernisation. Tradition, as an area of the aestheticisation of everyday life, as the production of the 'pretty', the 'charming', the 'picturesque' and 'exotic', is offered to the tourist in abundance by the last surviving 'locals' and the employees of the tourist offices.'

All peoples, as we know, have their own 'founding myth'; the official Swiss version is based on the legend of William Tell – a crude, violent, epic and warlike myth, which not even the artistic monumentalism of the great, popular national painter Ferdinand Hodler was able to bring to life. Nothing could be further from the neutral, peaceful Switzerland of today, with its occasional air of an enchanted garden. As with the Swatch and the Swiss cross, we might suggest a replacement here, too: instead of Tell's crossbow, perhaps a large bunch of red geraniums should become the symbol of Swiss quality! These flowers would refer to a second Swiss founding myth, more in keeping with contemporary mentality and the contemporary way of life: the myth of the tourist paradise, which links up and combines with that of the 'Belle Epoque'. After all, those secular cathedrals of the bourgeoisie, known as 'Grand Hotels' were the original home of the aestheticisation rites of everyday life that swept the country like a new morality, a new ethics, a set of values for a national identity tangible and visible down to the tiniest details.

7. Missionaries of Nostalgia

We should add that when it comes to the relationship between 'urban modernity' and 'rural mountain tradition', the voluntary associationism that thrives in Switzerland plays a principal role in the aestheticisation of everyday life. It creates a network of 'fundamental' relationships which permeates and informs all levels of everyday life. From philharmonic associations and choral societies to societies for the protection of mountain life, environmentalist groups, folk-dancing clubs, or associations of traditional Swiss wrestlers or alp horn players, it is difficult for a 'citizen' (however professionally involved in the most advanced fields of electronics or computer science) to avoid active participation in the production of nostalgia or the revitalisation of tradition.

At the beginning of our essay, we noted that Switzerland is a country which impressively confirms 'the twofold conceptual world of modernity' ('Franciscan-nostalgic' and 'Faustian-promethean') posited by Georges Auclair. The same might be said about the hypotheses and theories regarding multiple or nomadic identity as a prime characteristic of modernity, or more precisely of post modernity. More than any other country, Switzerland – whether at the individual or the collective level – exhibits the contradictory dualism between modernity/modernisation and nostalgia/tradition. But this does not seem to give rise to schizophrenia or an unhealthy sense of estrangement; rather, the Swiss manage to experience and master several contemporary identities at once, some of them shaped by the myths of the past, others by the adventure of the present and the future.

I should like nonetheless to add another brief example, or should we say metaphor: this time to stress that not everything connected with the relationship between an advanced level of modernity and the rural-pastoral tradition need find expression in a superficial, scenic simulation.

8. From the Stampa Valley to the Valleys of Paris

This new metaphor comes from the world of 'high culture'; more particularly, from a famous Swiss artist who died in the mid-1960s: the sculptor and painter Alberto Giacometti, who was born in Stampa, in the Bregaglia Valley of the Grisons, in 1901. I have long maintained that it is difficult to achieve a full understanding of Giacometti's modernity without taking into consideration his Swiss, Protestant roots and alpine origins; not to mention, of course, the transplantation of these elements to the cultural hothouse of Paris before and after World War II.

As his relatives and friends who still live in Stampa and nearby villages recount, Giacometti returned to Bregaglia Valley with great regularity, particularly in the last years of his life. He always came back in late autumn, when the sun no longer pierces the clouds above Stampa, and the snow has not yet released its brilliance on the valley floor like a fallen sky cast over the soft stretches of the meadows and slate roofs. The Bregaglia Valley is a sort of narrow, deep gorge in the midst of grey granite. Its geological darkness, its fractures and abrasions, fallen rocks and dizzying drops create megalithic monuments and temples to entropy, to the immanent fatigue of matter. This, more than anywhere else, is the place where – even before arrival at any of the legendary shrines of the Swiss tourist myth (such as Maloja or St Moritz) – the mountains evoke the drama, dark tragedy of those who were once compelled to live there. This is not a mountain that suggests vertical ascendance to heaven; with its erosions, fissures and alluvial cones, its deposits, moraines and abysses, it has the effect of a majestic, awe-inspiring landscape of disasters, ruins and debris. It is the mountain that at Sils Maria, a little higher than Stampa, conveys a message of madness far more convincingly through Nietzsche than communicable through its mere vertical thrust. And through Alberto Giacometti it gives us what may be the metaphor of a literally 'superhuman' weariness of life and death; an unbearable endurance of existence towards death, communicated to the inanimate and inorganic by the experience of pain. Well-acquainted with the nightmare of vertigo and the abyss, Giacometti wrote that Paris was very familiar to him because to him its dark, narrow streets resembled alpine valleys. And he would also write that in childhood two large, erratic blocks on the green slopes near the big house of Stampa, beyond the waterfall, had offered him the archetypal experience of the 'male' and 'female' principles so pervasive in his early works. One of them was black, jagged and compact; a surface that allowed no rest, no purchase, no foothold; neither rough nor porous and violently vertical at the same time. More than once it frightened away Alberto and his little friends. The other rock was grey, broad and irregular; full of footholds and clefts, it opened on one side in a long narrow cave; here Alberto used to crouch, sheltered from the world.

In short, would it be too much to assume that there is a certain 'Swissness' at the root of Alberto Giacometti's universality? That it expressed itself in an ineradicable need to come back to the harsh, primitive nature of his valley (whose granite-grey dominates his canvases) as a dynamic, dialectical counterpoint to the tempests of modernism?

The question leads us to venture a hypothesis concerning Swiss culture and its passage into modernity.

9. A Swiss Road into the Modern Age

When Switzerland is mentioned, non-Swiss tend to be puzzled that such advanced 'cultural phenomena' as those associated with Le Corbusier, Giacometti, Max Frisch, Friedrich Dürrenmatt, Max Bill, Jean Tinguely or Bernhard Luginbühl (to list only some of the better-known names) could emerge and take shape in a cut-off, dissociated social context excluded throughout the century from the great events of European and world history.

Switzerland is a nation which had been shielded, fortunately we might say, from the unprecedented tragedy of modern totalitarianism and two world wars that were to present civilisation with new and radical questions, shaking it to its very foundations. The lack of first-person, first-hand experience seems capable of creating a hiatus, a crucial gap: not only between 'Swiss culture' and the rest of the world, but even between that Swiss culture and modernity. The latter surely includes the last war, with all its horrors, which left that very modernity with a tormenting sense of guilt, a universally bad conscience. The tragic uniqueness and radical nature of that conflict – what might be called its 'anthropological inconceivability' and its barbaric thrust to the very heart of Western civilisation – meant that neutrality would necessarily appear as a loss of history, an irrevocable loss of the definition of the *condition humaine*. I am convinced that this loss of history permeates the whole of Swiss culture in the form of a loss of humanity and, temporarily, of modernity. Beginning as it does in the interwar years and continuing to the present day, it is unquestionably an indispensable key to our understanding of Swiss culture.

It is in my opinion this very loss that constitutes the tragic essence of a certain type of 'Swissness'; like a black hole, it seems to swallow up individual experience and the collective affective conceptual world, and results in radical existential plight. Both the great Swiss Expressionists (Ignaz Epper, Fritz Paul, Johannes Robert Schürch, Hermann Scherer, Otto Morach, etc.), and the *grande vague* of Swiss cinema in the 1960s (Alain Tanner, Michel Soutter, Claude Goretta, Daniel Schmid) depict it as quotidian bleakness.

The epicentre, or rather 'metastasis' of this 'Swissness' is Swiss everyday life, which appears to be a hyper-ritualised expression of history's twilight.

It is thus conceivable that Swiss culture also achieves access to modernity and postmodernity through this tragic aspect of everyday life. It might be said that the more everyday life is trapped in the repetitions of its own cyclical temporality and the recurrence of eternal sameness, the more quickly it is driven forward by the linear time of scientific and technological progress and the rationalising processes of production and consumption. Precisely because everyday life is affected by these processes, it appears to cloak the radical, frenzied, transformational processes of modernity in a mantle of continuity, of formal constants, 'resurrections', recreations and myths of the past. And all by means of a tireless aestheticisation of the immediate and the obvious.

It is almost superfluous to point out that, as a feature of the postmodern age, the extent and impact of this kind of everyday life is assuming ever greater dominance in the most scientifically and technologically advanced societies.

Alongside this structurally important lack of historical time, which has also been noted by Fabrizio Sabelli, there is a more obvious and familiar phenomenon that should not be ignored: the ambiguity, or diversity, of the ethnic, cultural and political identity of the Confederation. I am convinced that this oft-discussed fact has also helped to push Switzerland along the road to modernity. This mechanism has been becoming increasingly apparent over the past few years: cosmopolitanism as a way of levelling differences seems to be able to coexist, and even compete with the renaissance of all kinds of localistic and regionalistic ideas. And this coexistence, or contradictoriness, is emerging with ever greater clarity as a structural component of postmodernism itself.

From this point of view, too, Switzerland appears to have succeeded in finding a middle ground between modernity and tradition: in the unflagging simulation and miniaturisation of its already small national territory, but above all in the aestheticisation and enchantment of Switzerland's everyday life – which has visibly triumphed over existential plight and longing.

Rich Land, Poor Land – A Travel Report
Michael Rutschky

The code. In the plane flying from Berlin to Frankfurt – a mild day in early spring – the visitor is trying to concentrate on reading while the two young men next to him are engrossed in lively conversation. They are obviously not just colleagues but friends, going home to their families for the weekend. Young bankers, dressed like English gentlemen for cricket: white trousers, navy-blue sweater; only a pin-striped shirt still hints at their business uniform.

'There is no objective or absolute concept of poverty, nor one that might usefully be adopted from some other set of notions.' While the talk of the young bankers washes over the visitor, he is studying reports on poverty in Switzerland; during his tour of inspection he will pay especial attention to the aspects of wealth and poverty. 'Poverty is always a relational concept; to determine poverty requires the identification of two properties, opposites, or a difference.'

The visitor overhears the two young gentlemen complaining about a disastrous telephone network that complicates their business even more. The telephone network in East Berlin ... As far as the visitor can tell, they are with a bank that is setting up branch offices in the new Eastern Provinces of the Federal Republic of Germany. The rotten telephone network there is part of the legacy of socialism: chalk one up for Poverty.

The visitor is from a country that – at the time of his trip – is very busy grappling with the fact that it consists of two parts, one of which is poor in comparison to the other. In fact, there is such a gaping contrast between West and East that it overshadows the distinctions between rich and poor within each of them. And yet one needs only compare the two young gentlemen by the visitor's side to that petty bourgeoise over there – thick glasses, hard-lacquered hairdo, grown flabby in her misery – for those differences to stand out again.

On the other hand, western Germany has always been very reserved about showing its wealth. That elegant gentleman, for example, with his well-cut grey hair, in his delicately patterned suit, a silk ascot rather than a tie around his neck – the visitor knows he cannot be German even before he hears his upper class English.

Accompanied by a beautiful wife and daughter, the gentleman boards the plane to Zurich at Frankfurt. Several times the visitor feels the daughter's piercing glance, but – as he ruefully admits to himself – it is not elegance that attracts her attention but the fact that he is taking notes. A mystery surrounds someone writing in public. The notes observe that the elegant gentleman treats his wife and daughter with the utmost courtesy; this time Wealth has scored. Mythologically speaking, the three epitomise the shoppers on Bahnhofstrasse, Zurich's Fifth Avenue.

The People's Restaurant. In Bienne the visitor has an appointment with the director of the welfare office. In the station concourse he sees a beggar crouching on the ground. Poverty scores. He will be told time and again that the number of tramps has increased dramatically over the past few years. For society, beggars are a most gratifying embodiment of poverty. To the visitor, the native beggars seem particularly well-behaved and modest; there is not a trace of southern expressiveness in them.

Outside the station, the visitor comes upon damp, silver-grey weather and an obsession that will recur throughout his trip: he is struck by an uncanny resemblance between (wealthy) Switzerland and the (poor and abandoned) GDR, of all countries! During lunch, the welfare director unwittingly reveals why this applies to Bienne. The visitor meets her, an extremely pretty, delicate lady, at her office, in a forbidding building in the historicist style the Germans call 'Wilhelminian'. On the stairs he chalks up two points for Poverty: a Black with an embarrassed smile and a young alcoholic. For lunch, he was taken to the 'People's Restaurant', the director evidently unsettled because she is not quite sure what he wants from her. The visitor feels transported onto the set of a historical film, a large restaurant from the twenties. The high-ceilinged circular room is flooded with soft light from opaque white lamps – down with bourgeois dimness! The visitor learns that even in the '20s Bienne was a stronghold of the Social Democrats. In the '60s, when the watch industry was booming, great plans were made to improve the infrastructure. Bienne was to become the city of the social democratic future. But the boom receded, leaving ruins instead of projects. 'In 1966, 8,301 persons were employed in the Bienne watch industry,' the welfare director quotes from her papers, 'by 1984 the number of such jobs was down to 2,366. Unqualified workers, numerous women among them, were hardest hit by the redundancies.'

Four per cent of the population, the welfare director cautiously explains to the visitor as they consume their leg of ham and potato salad and sip their mineral water – four per cent of the population depends entirely on social security; add the people who receive supplementary benefits to augment income from other sources, and the figure jumps to ten per cent. This is a bitter parody on the ideology of the welfare state.

But this beautiful, historical room – the visitor gives it one last lingering look – will score a point for Wealth. In the former GDR it would long have been derelict or ruined by renovation. Perhaps one ought to say that Switzerland, even Switzerland in Bienne, is what the GDR would have liked to be.

Gradually the implications of this idea dawn on the visitor: it is not only (petty) bourgeois tidiness that the GDR has been yearning for; it is also Switzerland's capacity for self-centredness, because, basically, she does not look beyond her own borders (which the GDR, adjoined by such rich sisters, could never manage to do).

The welfare director explains to the visitor why political refugees are pushed back and forth; how few of them have left their countries for truly political reasons. – Does she cautiously drop her voice because she feels the tremendous burden of this problem? – Then she tells him something he will note for all future discussions: social work in the traditional sense, with its educational and therapeutic ambitions – this kind of social work is almost useless for helping clients solve their problems, even if it is only a matter of drawing up a budget. Not only do they learn nothing about making ends meet, but their spiritual needs remain unfulfilled as well. They need accountants to teach them how to be economical with limited means. This time Poverty scores because (economic) poverty has no legal status; it is still treated as a personal shortcoming or a weakness of character. Only at a higher level of civilisation do the poor receive simple charity – without being told what is wrong with their personality.

For the train ride from Bienne to Geneva the visitor has bought a tabloid; he wants to evaluate its Wealth/Poverty score. Somewhere out there, in the silvery waters of the lake, is the island of St Peter where Rousseau took refuge in 1765 from the inhabitants of Môtiers. Time has turned the island into a monument. One point for Wealth (cultural).
A city councillor was caught by shop detectives in the act of stuffing an expensive pair of pruning shears into the packaging of a cheaper pair: prosperity spawns this kind of petty offence.
A Swiss damsel spent fifteen years nursing a British millionaire for which he left her an enormous sum in his will. Such tales date from pre-modern times when wealth and poverty were dispensed according to the inscrutable whims of Fortuna. The Children's SOS Telephone Service notes an increase in calls of 45 per cent over the preceding year. The stories are terrible: a five-year-old girl has been locked up at home for three months; a six-year-old boy is continually beaten up; a seven-year-old girl's mother accuses her of having caused her breast cancer.
The visitor knows his own country's inclination to read such data as signs of a new social poverty ('child abuse' being only one of its many problems) that is not motivated by economic need – just as the councillor's theft of the shears was not motivated by hunger. But at least here the story was picked up by a tabloid.

Jewels. On entering his hotel room in rich and rainy Geneva, the visitor is again beset by his GDR-obsession: was it not there that he also saw such oddly tinted wallpaper, such ugly flowered bedspreads, such huge superfluous vases; and was it not there that the TV with its tiny screen was also placed much too far away from the settee? He muses that probably all European countries, regardless of their GNP and the standard of living, resemble the former GDR inasmuch as they do not suffer – as the 'old' FRG does – from the compulsion to construct new and renovate old buildings. A friend from the former GDR once told the visitor how surprised he was on his first visit to England. 'It looks just like Zwickau!' He found capitalist England much more akin to the GDR than to the FRG. Likewise, Geneva's wealth does not need to communicate itself in a permanent revolution of improvements and embellishments. Rather, its glow is natural, especially in those places where the city is a little shabby. There are plenty of people who consider West German perfectionism to represent a point for Poverty: people who are constantly compelled to make everything look like new have very little self-esteem.
The next day the weather is splendid, in the harsh sunlight the palaces of beautiful Geneva stand out with Italian clarity. The visitor strolls around – the lake, the tall jet of water: he has forgotten just how much it was part of the city's skyline. This place reminds the visitor intensely of the northern German city of Hamburg, also built around a body of water, the

so-called Binnenalster, on whose banks rise similar palace-like façades, and from which rises a similar jet. Here, as well as there, the scenery contains an element of fantasy that recalls historicising paintings of the nineteenth century – paintings like 'On the Waters of Babylon', or 'In the Port of Carthage: Dido Taking Leave of Aeneas'. The fantasy can be pursued: the city of dreams on the water once bowed to the commands of a theocrat, John Calvin.

'Even the slightest opposition to his views was suppressed, and the deeds, faces, and words of each inhabitant of Geneva were under close scrutiny.' Back home, this is what his ancient dictionary of 1888 tells the visitor. It also tells him that the tyrant was sad: 'His mood was usually melancholy and dark. If provoked by contradiction, his harsh and unrelenting disposition rose in bitter condemnation and proud disdain of those his keen mind unmasked and his spirit dominated.' Those who landed in this lovely harbour, says the fantasy, were ignorant of the horrors that lay ahead ...

But the palaces did not rise on the lake then; the streets looked like the ones in which the visitor is now strolling, the streets of the old city, around the Place du Bourg-de-Four, where the window displays of elegant shops make everything – food, books, clothing – look like precious jewels. (Some days later, in the arcades of Berne, the visitor will realise that the jewel-like displays are Swiss wealth incarnate.) Still later, in Lausanne, he will be told by a local that the hill on which the old city of Geneva is perched has been appropriated by the richest and most refined people, who even speak their own brand of French. With the utmost economy of lip-movement the local demonstrates it during their walk around hilly Lausanne – in the usual, silvery rain. After his return to Berlin, the visitor will find an announcement in his daily paper of the death of R. Duchess of B., born in 1921. 'Remembered in never-ending grief and gratitude,' by C. Duke of B., of an address on that hill in Geneva. The Internationale of Wealth. His ancient dictionary will tell him that the B.s were among the noblest families of the German empire, originally from Mecklenburg. They know how to choose a setting for themselves. Jewels even in this respect. – The visitor's imagination comes up with one last fantasy: If we agree with Max Weber, the famous German sociologist who saw the origins of capitalism in Calvinism, the theocrat should have been embalmed and put on display in a mausoleum on the Place du Bourg-de-Four – like Lenin on Red Square in Moscow ...

After a morning stroll through the old city of Geneva – already bathed in glorious sunshine – the visitor keeps his appointment with a sociologist.

Why has Switzerland become so wealthy? No one knows exactly. But two things are certain: it was once a very poor country, a country of peasants, and it may now well be the richest country in the world, says the sociologist as he rummages through his papers. In 1988, the GNP was 27,260 dollars per person – in Japan it was 21,040 dollars, in the U.S. 19,780 dollars. In the poorest countries – Mozambique, Chad, Ethiopia – the amount fluctuates between 100 and 160 dollars.

The sociologist goes on to mention that it is only in the past ten years that the existence of poor people in Switzerland (poor by Swiss standards, not by Chad's) has been more clearly recognised. And – the visitor speculates – it is a measure of a civilised society whether it allows its poor to be identified or whether it must insist that everybody is perfectly happy. There are countries that keep denying their periodical famines. Their governments refuse foreign aid, indignant of what they deem negative propaganda, or interference in their domestic affairs.

The sociologist is leafing through more papers. The problems in Switzerland are economic; it is not a matter of suicide rates, drugs or vagrants (attributed by some executives to 'new Poverty' – like child abuse). The poor – farmers, old people, mainly women and young couples with a low income starting a family – amount to either 3.2 or 11.4 per cent of the total population ('the exact figures aren't all that important') depending on whether the limit is set at an annual income of 8,936 or 13,900 Swiss francs.

No, the exact figures really are not that important. On a later, perfectly sunny day in Lucerne, a different expert on poverty will tell him why it is so difficult for the poor in Switzerland to recognise their own poverty and to reveal it to others. As yet, there is no legal right to claim welfare. One has to request it from one's community; and one's fellow citizens decide on whether one is entitled or not, whether one's income might be increased by, say, a paper run early in the morning. This can be extremely humiliating, especially in the country. The procedure by which a person's poverty is assessed belongs on the Poverty (social) scorecard, inasmuch as a richly socialised and civilised culture should have no need for such rituals of submission.

Along Lucerne's Seepromenade, whose sumptuous hotel palaces vie with those in Geneva, the visitor notes the names of the shops that look out on the lake. Watches Clocks. Hofstetter & Berney. Swiss Railway Travel Agency. Grieder (fashion). Watches Pendulen Uhren. Galerie du Quai. Antiquités. American Express. Hotel Schweizerhof. Danaya (fashion). Bookstore. Swiss Bank Corporation. Gübelin (watches and jewellery). Credit Suisse.

The following was also noted by the visitor during his talk with the sociologist in Geneva: 'He considers it part of the political and cultural wealth of Switzerland that her populations with their various idioms are not seriously concerned about their respective identities. Genevans quite naturally look to Paris, the alemannic Swiss to Germany, etc. If they were French, or German or Italian provinces, this would probably be much harder for them, for the Genevans would then be mere provincials, the alemannic Swiss mere south Germans, etc. At the same time, and without any national pathos, they pursue their own interests as Swiss. To reflect about one's identity is a kind of cultural poverty.'

Here I should add what the local in Lausanne explained to the visitor during their silver-grey, rainy stroll, what special feelings of inferiority the Vaudois nurse towards the rich Genevans and the Bernese who are in the political centre. But we will let the matter rest.

The visitor copied out the following letter to the editor of a daily paper: 'Comparing Switzerland with an Eastern country, or with the Gulf region, makes me realise that I'm living in a paradise. From now on, a Swiss flag will be flying from my balcony as a sign of gratitude. I would suggest that all my fellow citizens who appreciate our country fly the Swiss flag in the year of the anniversary, 1991. May this message reach the hitherto silent majority.' No doubt the GDR would have dearly loved to see her citizens display the same petty-bourgeois smugness about the socialist system. I think we have to give Poverty a point not for the complacency, but for its propagandist expression.

On the reservation. At the station of Erstfeld, wrapped in the mountains, the visitor is met by a deputy of the cantonal parliament who was owner of a hotel and the mayor here for a long time. They are going to visit the aborigines in their alpine valleys.

A thunderous storm fills the valley, and the air is so clear that every detail stands out even at a great distance. It is the *föhn*; according to the ancient encyclopedia, this is a 'warm, dry wind that generates extraordinary phenomena and sometimes blows in the middle ranges of the Swiss mountains.' Of especial note are the blue hues – we are witnessing a spectacle of nature that can score for Wealth insofar as it can only be seen here, in this place, like the volcanic eruptions that are unique to Hawaii.

Switzerland has long been exploiting this wealth, the market value of natural spectacles. As he is driven into Amsteg village in the deputy's car, the visitor notices a 'Tea Room'. In the nineteenth century, it was the English who discovered the natural delights of Switzerland. Later on, the American way established itself as the idiom of the culture. At Basle train station some days later, the visitor will observe two young men kissing each other's cheeks in traditional greeting – one of them is sporting a jacket whose emblem makes him out to be the member of a Californian baseball team.

But we are in Amsteg now. The visitor is given a room in a hotel in which Goethe, the poet, is said to have stayed (here, the transition from 'Wealth, natural' to 'Wealth, historical' is completely effortless). Later on, riding around in the deputy's four-wheel-drive Japanese car (according to the deputy, a model that is practically standard equipment for the locals), we are given a demonstration of poverty: damage caused by avalanches, especially bad because the protecting forests, weakened by various ailments, cannot hold back the snow; the motorway that vandalises the dramatic beauty of the valley (and damages the forests); the hotel industry that has suffered a great deal because of the Gotthard road tunnel which saves tourists bound for Italy a stop in the valley. 'This avalanche shelter is ancient; even Goethe described it.' They are standing outside; it is so warm that the visitor has left his coat in the hotel. Then things become serious. While the gently swaying car of a cable railway pulls them up the steep mountainside, the visitor – nursing his fear of heights – anxiously studies the steeply sloping pastures he will have to climb down on foot afterwards. The deputy loves his natives, extols their way of life, feels responsible for them. He keeps telling the visitor how cheerful alpine farmers are, how healthy their complexion, how strong and agile they are: the wiry man who meets them at the second farm, how nimbly he negotiates the steep slope as he shows them to his house – he is over 70! And the hospitality – always serving a snack the moment their guests have settled in the parlour – bread, butter,

a whole cheese, a plate of freshly cut bacon and the beverage everybody cautioned him about before he had even left Lausanne: *Kaffee-Schnapps*, weak, sugary coffee with a generous dash of spirits.

The deputy regaled the visitor with stories of how he came to the rescue of aborigines living on the brink of disaster. How he organised helicopters to supply snow-bound families with the basic necessities – comforters for a mother whose baby couldn't stop crying. Though desperate, she could barely bring herself to ask for them, embarrassed by the extravagance of using a helicopter for such a trifle. I was told how he had managed to persuade the rich in Zurich and other cities to make donations, to sponsor families, to fund foundations. That particular family desperately needed water mains; in fact the whole derelict house – the deputy's chin begins to tremble – was renovated for the young woman living in such isolated circumstances with her three children. Then there are the ballads: The beautiful maid who had to renounce the most handsome young man in the whole valley. She locked herself into the room at the top of her parents' house, never to leave it again, her two sisters looking after her for 60 years. When her beloved died and they carried his coffin down the valley, they saw her in the window, a spectral, silvery-white apparition … 'She was enraptured,' says the deputy, 'enraptured.' Pleasantly stimulated, or lulled, by the alcohol, the visitor scrambles down the steep slopes. Not a trace of vertigo. At times, there is a drizzle or a gentle flurry of snow.

The alpine farmers raise cattle for a living; the state guarantees the prices and there are extra premiums and subsidies.

They can eke out an existence as long as there is no disastrous unexpected expense. The alpine farmers, like other indigenous peoples, seem to nurture unusually strong ties to their land; to work it, to live where their ancestors lived, even under the most miserable conditions – one homestead shown to the visitor had no chimney, since time immemorial the kitchen has been covered with a strong-smelling, black layer of soot. The alpine farmers have a deeply rooted sense of tradition. Life is supposed to go on as it always has; modern things – the visitor saw TV sets, a mass-produced portrait of the Pope, a bottle of Oil of Olaz, a sticker 'I (heart) Schächental' – are quietly incorporated into the traditional lifestyle.

The deputy points to the landscape gardening which the farmers practise to stave off ecological disasters: if they did not repair the effects of winter erosion, which are visible everywhere, the mountains would come sliding down into the valleys. The deputy's enthusiasm for his people reminds the visitor of his obsession: the GDR would have loved to see this devotion in all her party secretaries. Outwardly, the deputy says, the alpine farmers seem poor, but they are blessed with great inner wealth. The visitor understands; they bear within themselves something like the pure gold of Helveticity.

Miniature models. In beautiful and wealthy Basle, the visitor received a dark intimation of poverty. It was in a cheap department store where, as he could see immediately, all the leather purses – the devil knows why he looked at them at all – were made of plastic, and where an ancient woman, stiffly looking at the ground through thick glasses, was creeping along the aisle on crutches. This would have been all right if there had not been a sudden mixture of odours: from the body of a fattish young saleswoman, from the cheap perfume sold on the left, and from the frying oil of a snack-bar on the right – grilled sausage with a soggy roll. Unlike money, poverty stinks.

At the Kunsthalle, the visitor sees a retrospective of the French artist Robert Filliou, member of the Fluxus movement, an avant-garde artist of the '50s. They preferred the cheapest materials: brown paper, plywood, rags, noise, nonsense – not a bad indication of the wealth of a country, of the world to which they belong. In a poor world, the works of art have to be made of gold leaf, ultramarine, they must be like jewels, precious, sumptuous symbols of power. In the GDR, the visitor once saw an exhibition inspired by Joseph Beuys' aesthetics (he was also a member of Fluxus). All it took was a glance out of the window at the garbage heap into which socialism was turning to come closer to Beuys. *Arte povera* presupposes a context of extreme wealth.

With its Filliou exhibition, the Basel Kunsthalle entered the ranks of the Internationale of Wealth, just as Geneva did with its Duke of B. In Zurich, the visitor will admire an exhibition of '80s design, showing flyers and posters of the anarchistic youth movement of the early '80s juxtaposed with commercial posters and magazine designs that immediately exploited the tantalising poverty of those demonstrations – in a mechanism similar to that at work in *Arte povera* …

After a look round the Filliou exhibition, the visitor went to the elegant Kunsthalle restaurant where he had one of those salads composed – as if to extend artistic pleasure – of inconspicuously expensive ingredients which also grace the menus in his own country. At the neighbouring table, he notes a young man with wild hair, wearing jeans and a t-shirt, drinking beer and avidly studying a book from the '70s on social revolutions.

What would that young man have had to say about Filliou? He would have written off the Zurich movement's dénouement in the lap of luxury as 'exploitation' and 'marketing', and probably given the visitor an incendiary lecture on the new poverty in wealthy Switzerland. The subsequent exchange between visitor and waiter could have been designed as grist for the young man's mill: having asked for the lavatories the visitor was told that they were accessible only from the restaurant. The street door was locked, because of the mainliners, as the waiter calls them, who would immediately take over the bathrooms. How typical, the social-revolutionary young man might moan. But that's not it, the drug scene is not typical of the new poverty in this wealthy country. The visitor has learned that he will meet the poor in the street later on, but – old or young – he will be unable to identify them. In Basel, he was also sent to the Mustermesse, a trade fair that would be instructive as a small scale model of consumer Switzerland.

Not an experienced fair-goer, the visitor meandered through the exhibition halls, slightly numbed, uncertain of what – if more closely studied – might reveal an allegory of Helvetian wealth, Helvetian poverty.

He finally pocketed the brochures from a timber-frame construction firm. They were selling the same type of houses the visitor had seen in the mountains when he was with the natives, only much smaller and for an entirely different purpose.

Houses of natural wood, for animals. Healthy homes for beloved pets. Carefully adapted to the animals' habits, special interiors for small animals. Houses for ducks, chickens, dogs. Houses for bees. Houses for sheep, goats. Stables for ponies and donkeys.

And chalet letter boxes: beautifully crafted in natural wood 44 mms thick, wind and weather-proof, finished with three coats. Floor models and wall models. Models for flats: a house for letters to people living in flats, with shingle or copper roof; disposal stations for containers or rubbish bins of all kinds, detached or semi-detached to suit existing house fronts, with a wide variety of colour options and available with built-in notice board or built-in letter box. The miniature Swiss chalet to camouflage the garbage container and house the letter box: an index fossil for the petty bourgeoisie with its own Internationale.

I am no longer sure why I was so affected by those objects. For one thing, there was the screamingly comic contrast between their solemn solidity and the plywood installations in the Kunsthalle.

And the fact that I take pleasure in such comparisons makes me a member of the 'professional middle class', special section 'intelligentsia'. It has always been a favourite pastime of the intelligentsia – whose roots are in the petty bourgeoisie – to score the latter group's clumsiness and its passion for kitsch as 'Poverty, cultural'. The Swiss damsel I read about on the train from Bienne to Geneva, whose faithful services were so richly rewarded by her lord – back in her native country, she will add the final touch to her newly acquired farm in Burgdorf: a chalet for the barnyard pets. Laughter.

But let us imagine the young saleswoman and the young office worker who can barely afford the price of admission to the Mustermesse. No chance of buying their small child an ice-cream, however piercingly it whines. The riches on show are only for the eyes – no thought of a house of their own; not even the smallest swimming pool is within their grasp. That they should have compatriots who can afford it all, plus a letter box of natural wood, with a shingle-roof, made to order – tears of helplessness prick the young woman's eyes. Poverty is a matter of context.

Switzerland in Europe: Towards the Year 2000

Claude Imbert (*Le Point*, Paris) and Daniel Vernet (*Le Monde*, Paris)
in conversation with Antoine Maurice (*Journal de Genève*).

Antoine Maurice (AM): When talking about the future of Switzerland we have to look at the country's assets and its handicaps. Switzerland's assets lie first and foremost in the economic field: Switzerland's industry is competitive and export-oriented. It is a communication centre, strategically situated in the heart of Europe. The country's location is, in fact, one of the big headaches in its relationship with the European community because of such issues as alpine transit.

Switzerland is still an important – albeit controversial – centre of international finance, although nowadays, when people talk about the country, it almost sounds as if they were talking about intestinal problems, as if Switzerland were a constipating factor in Europe.

Nevertheless, it has achieved a high degree of integration, real integration, within the European Community's economic mechanisms. This is true of both banking and industry. Major Swiss industries, much more than smaller and middle-sized ones, have already made their dispositions within the economic reality of the Community with great thoroughness, to the extent that some people have made it quite clear that it would not be a particular problem for them if the Confederation were to join the Community.

Switzerland is a country in which social peace and peace in industrial relations was and still is considered exemplary. This reality is part of the country's political culture; it is based on elaborate – and delicate – social consultation mechanisms and we cannot assume that it will last for ever.

Finally, perhaps because of its traditional love of nature and the myths associated with the landscape, it is a country in which environmental questions played an important role rather earlier than they did in the rest of Europe, although with certain reservations. It is a place where companies feel that they can set up factories with pleasant conditions for their employees, but at the same time face restrictive and complex injunctions concerning the environment at the three decision-making levels – commune, canton and Confederation.

Switzerland's primary political asset is that it belongs to that very small group of highly developed democracies characterised by strong popular participation. Local people participate actively in community life and this is the cornerstone of Swiss federalism. Compromise and consensus have become genuinely national characteristics. Federalism has been considerably shaken by technical and economic developments in recent years, but it is still a worthwhile point of reference. Politically, Swiss society is more or less middle-of-the-road in present-day Europe, in other words, the ideological debate – although eschewed by the highly pragmatic Swiss – oscillates between a position of Christian Democracy and well-tempered Social Democracy. In this respect, as in others, Switzerland is normal in comparison with neighbouring countries.

Let us briefly enumerate Switzerland's handicaps. Clearly there is the question of its neutrality which many Swiss people have come to consider a mythical burden that is very hard to bear. The myth of neutrality and sovereignty, and the way we define ourselves in an international context as a special case, dies hard and has a slightly narcissistic quality. This is a handicap not only in terms of negotiations with Europe, but also in a larger perspective than the commitment to the European Community. Switzerland's special brand of direct democracy would be considerably upset by entry into the Common Market, as a large number of laws that are at present subject to popular vote would no longer be so.

Finally Switzerland has a history – think of World War II and its attitude then – that could be a problem for some.

Is Switzerland suffering from an image problem among its partners, particularly among its larger neighbours, and if so, how does that affect the debate on joining the Common Market?

Claude Imbert (CI): I don't know if we know, even if the Swiss themselves know, exactly what Switzerland is. But in any case a number of countries have an idealised perception of Switzerland. In Europe at least, Switzerland has become a democratic eldorado by virtue of indisputable facts: its neutrality, the high economic standards and its political acumen – the 'sea of calm'. A second argument and one which also contains an element of myth, is that Switzerland, because of what for a long time was absolute protection of banking secrecy and the absence of inflation, has become a refuge for money. For a country like France, which – unlike other countries – has had interminable periods of exchange control, Switzerland also has the image of being a slightly wicked refuge. 'A Swiss bank account' is an expression that has become part of contemporary language; you will hear it in French songs and any bistro you might go into. Like all collective images some of these have a grain of truth. Others are drawn from clichés. On the whole, the balance is in favour of the Swiss. Besides, when questionnaires try to establish the popularity of foreign countries, Switzerland effortlessly comes out on top. But I think that the reason for its coming out on top is based on the image people have of it.

If one goes a little beyond this popular image, there is among better educated French people a kind of approval, even admiration of the way in which the Swiss have resolved the following mystery: how can a country with three great European cultures and three great languages manage to live a seemingly harmonious collective life without any apparent major tensions, to the point of forming a nation that is historically solid and steady? It is a question that considerably intrigues the French who, as you know, are inclined to be Jacobinian and not particularly federalist in their traditions. Another intriguing mystery is – or was – the intense patriotism of the Swiss. Many French people, even if they know very little about Switzerland, are aware of its unusual military system and the rigorous military obligations imposed on Swiss men, and the French are impressed by the personal sacrifice that such military duty entails. French people who think about it are intrigued by the fact that such exacting patriotism can unite men of such different cultures, at least this is how things were sometimes seen in recent decades. Today, even if these ideas, these images, these clichés are still remembered, people who are somewhat better informed are a little perturbed by something they see as a certain crisis in Swiss values. The referendum on the army has shaken French ideas about

Swiss patriotic sentiment. In the same way the passion of some Swiss intellectuals (Dürren-matt, Frisch, etc.) for torpedo-ing certain collective values has made a powerful impression on members of the French intelligentsia.

In fact, personally, I have always thought that Swiss political acumen contains a certain ingredient of something that could all too easily be called 'hypocrisy' , which in my opin-ion is an important factor for democratic success in a federal system. I think that what we call 'hypocrisy' is one of the essential ingredients of consensus. By 'hypocrisy', I mean that differences are minimised or reduced to tolerable levels in order to emphasise areas of agreement. It also means not worrying about abstract or intangible truths, but subordinat-ing them to the modest pragmatism of collective relationships. I think I can detect a new trend in Swiss society and particularly among young people. They show greater interest in abstract truth and much less in the constraints of consensus, and they condemn hypocri-sy, especially as a form of social politeness. In brief, the cohesive elements are a little less united than they used to be.

Daniel Vernet (DV): Elements of myth are very firmly anchored in Swiss reality. We would have to break down this general image and see whether everything that has just been said applies in the same way to all the cantons and to all levels of society. But fundamentally I have the impression that as far as this slightly mythical image is concerned a certain normal-isation can be discerned: it seems to me that Switzerland is becoming more and more Euro-pean. Various events illustrate this phenomenon. The first, which is anecdotal or even folk-loric, is the fact that a woman was elected minister for the first time a few years ago. Then there is the fact that there have been political scandals, that the Swiss economy can no long-er function without inflation and without unemployment – although the percentages are not as high as in other European countries. At the same time the myth of Swiss banks has not exactly collapsed, but it has at least been seriously shaken over the last ten years by various laws, measures and regulations. Then there's the fact that *Chaoten* (anarchist hooligans), squatters, etc. have been seen in the streets of Zurich and other large Swiss cities, and the fact that drugs have put in a spectacular appearance in Swiss towns, not in the form of banks laundering drug money, but because there are young people shooting up in the parks, etc. Claude Imbert mentioned the army. Switzerland is also being scrutinised, at least by those who govern it and by its intellectuals and journalists, in short by anyone who has something to say about the development of society, questions about Europe and what Switzerland will become within this Europe. It really seems to me that Switzerland is becoming more like any ordinary European country, that it is becoming increasingly absorbed into a general process of evolution. Its status as an island of prosperity, as a protected island, is gradually disap-pearing, or at least being questioned.

A.M.: And what would be the cost of integration?

D.V.: I don't think the economic cost would be very great. As far as agriculture is concerned, things will perhaps be very difficult for Switzerland, but I don't think there will be any real problems for the financial and industrial sectors. On the other hand, there will be political casualties, for example, loss of sovereignty and of the ability to change laws by referendum.

These losses are quite heavy and will be all the heavier the longer Switzerland waits to join or at least to apply to join and become involved in the process that will one day lead to membership. Switzerland risks being faced with a Europe that is already integrated. Personally, though I may be wrong, I don't think that any setbacks in the next few months could stop the Europe of the twelve moving forward. The process may be slowed down, it may take longer than we thought, but it will not be halted. And so Switzerland will inevitably have to face this problem and the longer it waits, the more difficult integration will be.

A.M.: Do you think that problems could arise for other European countries and France because of Switzerland's stance during the World War II? Is there a shadow that has remained because Switzerland was neutral?

C.I.: I don't think that the French found neutrality as discreditable as some Swiss seem to find it today in retrospect. Everyone can identify the various services that Swiss neutrality was able to offer to many different people. There is probably even a general desire that this kind of island of neutrality should continue to exist so that in the case of major conflicts there is a place available in which adversaries can at least speak to each other.

What astonishes me is that this question should be raised in the context of a discussion about whether Switzerland should or should not join the European Community, as if to imply that Switzerland should be full of complexes about its neutrality in the last war now that it is faced with the challenge of a changing Europe. In fact the present structure of Europe unites countries like France, Germany, Italy and England who were ferocious opponents in World War II. All these countries are clearly trying to get over something that happened over 45 years ago and on the whole they are succeeding. The question of Swiss neutrality is certainly important, but only as far as its future role is concerned in a Europe tending towards a common foreign policy and above all a common defence policy. However, the ancient fact that Switzerland was neutral in the last war does not seem to me to play any specific part in the way in which other Europeans see Switzerland today.

Let me say in passing that what intrigues us is Switzerland's current identity crisis, this way of questioning things that seem secure and that used not to be discussed. I have read articles in some magazines from French-speaking Switzerland laden with guilt feelings like those of the French left in the '50s.

A.M.: I should like to return to the concept of neutrality and, more generally, to the position that Switzerland could take up in international affairs. Here we find a modesty that in the eyes of some citizens is excessive, but which has found a kind of 'niche', to use a marketing term, that it now shares with other countries. This is manifested in an open attitude to the world – as is proved by its economic relationships – and in a cultivation of tolerance. It is also reflected in its capacity not only to furnish material help to accommodate international conferences and the European headquarters of the United Nations, but also to provide an impetus in resolving international problems. This has always been the tradition and today, faced with Europe on the move, I often have the impression that our leaders no longer find it so easy to follow this path. Does it seem to you that in Europe, as it is currently changing, there is still room for this attitude and, more broadly, for neutrality as we understand it?

D.V.: One ought to write a kind of historical survey of neutrality. Swiss neutrality could be analysed or defined as the will not to be part of the larger blocs that have been created on the continent of Europe or in the world: the Hapsburg Empire, the Russian Empire, the British Empire, the French Empire in the late 19th and early 20th centuries; in the years between the wars, Bolshevism, rising Nazism and the western democracies; after the war it could be seen as a desire not to choose between East and West. This non-participation was necessary to leave, not an empty space, but a neutral one to permit meetings – some indirect – between the Resistance and the Vichy regime, between Algeria and France during the Algerian war, between Reagan and Gorbachev, etc.

Today this need is fading. Without the antagonism between East and West since the collapse of the communist system, being neutral means not participating, but not participating in what? This is one of the fundamental problems that Switzerland has to face, because this neutrality, the refusal to join the United Nations, for example, does not really make sense. It was comprehensible when it was a matter of saying that Switzerland was neither in the Western or the Soviet camp, nor a non-aligned country like those of the Third World and thus nowhere. That does not make sense any more.

A.M.: Something else occurs to me. Provided that the great powers recognise this posture of impartiality, Switzerland can draw upon a humanitarian tradition. Switzerland's foreign policy owes a great deal to the tradition of the ICRC, the International Committee of the Red Cross – and vice versa. Do you think that abandoning neutrality will prejudice that tradition? Might it not be necessary to preserve both?

D.V.: The humanitarian tradition should certainly be preserved. Abandoning neutrality would not necessarily prejudice this tradition – which has had its ups and downs – as the two are not necessarily linked indivisibly. When I say 'ups and downs' I am thinking of the role played by the ICRC on certain occasions. It could be a bit like Switzerland in World War II: you could always find this or that person who sympathised with the Third Reich and others who favoured the opposite camp. This is why I speak of 'ups and downs', but this is not fundamental and it does not alter my general evaluation of Switzerland's attitude.

A.M.: Anyway, whatever hypothesis you follow, is neutrality a principle that we can do without and that must be sacrificed?

D.V.: Most certainly, at least one form of neutrality. But there too you have to use your imagination a little.

A.M.: If you are a member of a political union and that union has a common foreign policy, however narrowly or broadly it is defined, you are a member of an alliance and consequently there is no longer any room for neutrality.

D.V.: Absolutely. But this is leading us a little way into the realms of political fiction as no one really knows what form Europe will take in the next ten years. I can well imagine that the members of this developing European community will enjoy different levels of obligation both in terms of economic development and their different political systems, and that not all of them will be constrained by the same foreign and defence policies. That could easily happen. To that extent there could be a place for a certain kind of neutrality, a certain heritage of neutrality; for example, the heritage of humanitarian organisations.

A.M.: I should like to know what you think about the state of European integration. For as long as we have been observing it from the outside, we have always had the impression that there is a tendency to oscillate, practically from one day to the next, between moments of black pessimism, of Euro-pessimism – throughout the '80s there was a feeling in the air that everything was going to fail – and sudden new constructive phases of revitalised integration. Now the prospect has emerged of a revision of the Treaty of Rome in terms of two extremely ambitious projects, and to us Swiss, rightly or wrongly, it seems to be absolutely inevitable. Should we allow ourselves to be guided by this and say that it would be better to try to participate in this monetary and political union, since they seem to have a chance of making progress, rather than staying outside and having no possibility as a small country of a voice at all?

D.V.: I think there are two ways of looking at things: since we are undoubtedly moving in the direction of closer and closer European union, Switzerland ought to be involved in this process in one way or another, as all the other European countries wish to be, whether they are Switzerland's EFTA partners or the new democracies of Eastern Europe. Everyone wants to be involved in this particular European Community, at least as far as its economic implications are concerned, and it is hard to see how Switzerland could stay outside for long. In theory Switzerland has understood very well that it is in its interest to be involved in this group and to benefit from the advantages associated with such involvement.

There is also the problem of resurgent nationalism in Europe and this problem could also affect Switzerland one day. The movement towards European integration could well be accompanied by a resurgence of particular national and regional characteristics. In this respect it is quite interesting to hear what the Slovaks are saying: one of the arguments for separating from the Czechs runs like this:'Anyway it doesn't matter much if Slovakia is independent as we're all going to be together in a great integrated Europe.' One can imagine Ticino saying the same thing tomorrow: 'What difference does it make whether we are independent from Switzerland or not since we'll be integrated into a larger Europe with all the other cantons?' This is perhaps a somewhat theoretical consideration, but it is a question that could crop up one day.

Then there is another question associated with the definition of Europe. What is Europe? For years, in France, Germany and elsewhere, people have tended to speak of Europe when they were really referring to the European Community; first it was the European Economic Community, then the European Community, before you were thinking of the six, then the nine and now the twelve. Now when Europe is mentioned you have to be careful: is it this Europe of the twelve or is it Europe as a geographical reality? By this I mean that the Community and the leaders of its member countries have for years thought in terms of the political and economic integration of Western Europe.

Since 1989 we have been confronted with another dimension: the opening up of Europe, the abolition not of frontiers, but certainly of the one long frontier that used to cut Europe in two.

And it has to be said that we are somewhat uncertain in the face of this development. We are by no means ready to respond to this challenge, which represents a resurgence of nationalism, and involves both countries that are definitely pursuing democracy and others that are in extremely dubious political situations. There is some reason to fear that they could suddenly start to undermine the very foundations of European integration, which have been established by 30 years of work. I think reasons beyond its control, you might call them historical accidents, have placed Switzerland at the centre of this question, without its necessarily wanting to be. For the response to the demand for integration on the part of Switzerland, Austria and the other EFTA countries could well be a signal to Czechoslovakia, Poland, Lithuania and other countries.

C.I.: It is fundamental to remember that the countries within the Community of the twelve do not by any means see Europe in the same perspective. It seems to me that if I were Swiss I would say: 'Since the face of Europe is going to change radically in the future, let's wait and see what happens.' It seems to me that the Swiss are convinced that the movement towards European integration is going to proceed in a linear fashion and quite rapidly. I would tend to think in the same way, but I am not absolutely convinced. For we have arrived at a point where it is no longer a matter of improving economic integration. What has to be done is a leap into a new configuration and that will be a political one. This represents a considerable change in the nature of things, and it will radically transform the relationship of member states to the new European entity.

A.M.: You seem to have the impression, at least to a certain extent, that the European Community will continue as the privileged centre of initiative and energy within a European cluster, but that it will still certainly suffer from the backlash of the enormous upheavals that are going on in the East.

C.I.: That will certainly have the effect of slowing things down.

D.V.: Yes, but that does not resolve Switzerland's problems about the structure of Europe and the European Community. Switzerland has to make up its mind about what it wants to do. There are not an awful lot of options: EFTA belongs to the past and I doubt that the European Economic Area as such is going to last for very long. Whatever qualitative leap the European Community makes in the coming months, Switzerland has to consider participating in or at least defining, the nature of its links with this Europe of the twelve.

C.I.: I repeat that I have a feeling that at the moment Switzerland is moving rapidly and strongly. I think it is remarkably innovative when, for example, a Swiss member of parliament says: 'We must let the consensus system yield to the system of majorities and minorities.' We have come to believe – perhaps to an excessive extent – that what made the Confederation so solid was precisely that it was able to reach a consensus rather than following a system of alternating forces.

A.M.: I think that the prospect of joining Europe has provoked a questioning mood, a kind of shock that is running through the Swiss social and political body. There is a certain fear that all the old values, all those resources that we have just listed, are at risk of being subverted by entry into Europe in general and the European economic area in particular. Now, there is a fundamental paradox to be resolved in this questioning of the value, the quality of the Swiss model. Certain friends have been telling us for a long time that it represents a sum of experience which one day could be of use, in some way or other, in the building of Europe.

C.I.: I'm inclined to think that it was the very fact of the strong cultural differences and their acceptance as such that brought about an 'excess' of Swiss patriotism, a mental effort instilled in citizens and accepted by them as necessary. This mental effort consisted of inventing national patriotism, superimposed on the expression of each of the cultural identities existing in Switzerland. I have always thought that the Swiss have internalised their awareness of the fragility of the Confederation and its conglomerate of highly heterogeneous cultures, so that in order to protect themselves against this fragility the Swiss invented this strong patriotic cement without which the heterogeneous blocks would not hold together.

D.V.: In fact I think one has to distinguish two levels. First of all there is the thing that defines the nature of Switzerland, in other words this conglomerate of different cultures, languages, religions and people who, despite their differences, have the feeling of belonging to the same entity: this has always been and still is a unique characteristic of Switzerland. But suppose Switzerland does enter Europe some day; a Europe organised in a totally different way, where languages, regions and local characteristics acquire much greater significance than they have now. It really makes one wonder whether the notion that a Switzerland that is special and different from other nations might not be outweighed at that point by the attraction of the language and culture particular to each of the populations that make up Switzerland. It really is a fundamental question. Then there is the level of politics and consensus, a level that I think is a little different. It is perfectly possible to imagine that this cohabitation of languages and cultures might function with a parliament and a government that is a little more confrontational than the one we have known since the coalition between Christian Democrats, Radical Democrats and Social Democrats that has existed for more than 30 years now. It is even possible to imagine that Switzerland could exist without this coalition!

There is another question, if I have understood your discussion on constitutional mechanisms correctly, about the structure of government: the Federal Council could be organised differently, there could be a prime minister . . . And it seems to me that it is not entry into Europe that provokes questions about the present system. It is the very idea that Switzerland might one day enter Europe that has stimulated the discussion about the current system. Merely addressing the problem of Switzerland's relationship with Europe necessitates revaluating the function of the Federal Council as it has existed since 1959. This is extraordinary and Switzerland is not even in Europe yet. What will happen when it is?

A.M.: Isn't Europe looking for more political consensus – at which point the Swiss model would still be interesting – or is there an urgent need for a little more opposition?

A well-functioning democracy is a little like electricity: two relatively clearly placed poles are needed for the citizens. But Switzerland is somewhat different because the system consists of extremely fine gradations ranging from centre-right to centre-left. Would it not be a good idea, as Daniel Vernet suggested, to think about a more parliamentary form of government that would give a little more weight to the opposition? Would this be desirable or not?

D.V.: The model upon which Europe is presently built is to some extent the Swiss model – though much diluted. But in the end the way in which the Council of Ministers, the Community and the Parliament function perhaps approaches this model. The problem is that a time will come – and it seems to me that Switzerland has already reached this threshold – when decisions can no longer be made with this model. Or when the range of choices has been depleted. This might be said to apply to Switzerland as far as Europe is concerned. The Swiss government is faced with a fundamental choice of major importance for the future of the country. A choice which could have very serious consequences for the cohesion of the cantons and the working of the system. To a certain extent the compensatory mechanisms that have always functioned will turn out to be paralysing.

C.I.: It is clear that the Swiss system offers all the advantages (and the inconveniences) offered by a proportional rather than a majority system. The organisation of communal life, as you said in your introduction, is very rich. Inside the little cell of a small community the responsibilities seem much better distributed than in a community of the same type in France. The Swiss system involves the citizen much better in everything concerned with public life, from the local community to the canton. But at the same time, and here I agree with Daniel Vernet, it seems that action is almost paralysed by proportionalism and the consensus system as far as major national political decisions are concerned.

A.M.: Another field is the relationship between North and South. Here Switzerland could possibly have a role to play, though it would certainly be a modest one. But because there are several specialised United Nations institutions on its territory and a large number of non-governmental organisations, it could take on one of the roles that you mentioned before. It is small, and could also play the part of devil's advocate. It also has the good fortune of having a system which prevents major decisions from being taken quickly. It can take the risk of waiting, because present-day Europe is moving centripetally in a way that is bound to provoke an opposing current. There is inevitably going to be a movement towards the regions or towards the periphery. So why not wait? In fact this calculation is being made in Switzerland, you often hear it said: 'They are going to fall apart anyway, so let's wait!'

D.V.: I do not think these two movements are contradictory, on the contrary, a tendency to create micro-states is paradoxically part of European unification. I have quoted the Slovaks, but if one takes the Slovenes and the Croats, they certainly want independence, but at the same time they desire integration into the European Community because they want to be part of a larger group. What they don't want any longer is large nations.

C.I.: We should also speak of Switzerland's relatively small population. In its present form its political and economic weight is much greater than its demographic weight, whereas in a larger group there might be concern that the specific weight of Switzerland would be more in proportion to the size of its population.

A.M.: But even so, the principle of federalism, of which the European organisation is a sort of avatar, means that small entities are over-represented in relation to large ones, which is, we are always told, in favour of our membership. So far we have only talked about Europe. But what do developments on the Old Continent mean in the eyes of South America, Africa and Asia?

C.I.: It is possible to imagine that Switzerland – if it is to become a well-integrated part of the European Community – could lose some of its unusual qualities. If the question that you are asking is: 'How would this look to someone in Phnom Penh or Rio de Janeiro or an American in Washington?' it seems to me that one could reply in all three cases that they would not see Switzerland as Switzerland, but as a little nation in Europe. The Dutch, for example, because of their language, have something that will remain their own. But the risk is greater for countries like Switzerland whose languages are European languages from much more populous countries: Germany, Italy and France. They risk having more difficulty in preserving their own identity within larger linguistic groups. It seems to me that language is all the more important in terms of holding people together as the old political structures are shaken by the present European upheavals.

D.V.: Many Swiss – even if they are not all multilingual – have an opportunity that not everyone has in Europe: that of speaking or at least being exposed to several European languages – Italian, French, German (and English). This is not the case for everybody and probably, if we do not wish Europe to be exclusively English-speaking, Europeans will in future have to master several of those languages. The problem of determining whether Switzerland would lose some of its image is not very important in the face of Europe's potential ability to shape a policy for the South, for the Mediterranean, Africa and Latin America. For some years it has been clear that the European Community exists much more for the outside world than Europeans themselves are aware. This is true of the European countries that are not part of it, but it is equally true of non-European countries, whose questions and expectations far exceed what Europe can do or offer in its present form.

A.M.: But surely the concept 'nation' will be modified?

C.I.: I am inclined to say that it is necessary, throughout Europe, to concern ourselves with what a nation is when confronted with this new type of organisation, because, if we do not pay attention to the nation, it will leap at our throats. If we do not foster a healthy dose of nationalism, then reactionary nationalist feeling will rear its ugly head. The demand for nationhood has two faces: it contains both peace and conflict. What is the fate of the nation in Western Europe? No one knows. Will it be diminished by the phenomenon of the new community? Or will it be reinforced by its revival in Eastern Europe? Perhaps politics will be redefined? I mean the relationship of citizen to state. In France we still have a kind of over-representation of national sentiment in the sense of a persistence or revival of a kind of Bonapartist monarchism and all this is supported by the present constitution, which has many advantages for a country that is difficult to govern. From this point of view the Swiss model does not seem passé to us French, but rather more modern. The relative and actually practised modesty of Swiss political practice seems close to what many citizens would like in a country like ours today.

A.M.: To some extent all the more, as a small country could enhance its influence.

D.V.: It is not only the question of a small country or a big country. What is a small country or a big country? It involves demographic thrust, but also cultural, linguistic and economic influence. It is very easy to see how the balance of power is going to be created in Europe and how it would be created if there was no European Community and if there was not this structure that has been functioning, after a fashion, for a little over 30 years. For us, Europe is not a substitute for a nation, a fatherland, etc. as it has been for generations of Germans, up to and including today. This is not at all the case in France. But I think that people are becoming aware that they are confronted with a scenario of international relationships in which the nation-state inherited from the 19th century can no longer play the part that it played up to World War II. It is therefore necessary to create forums through which traditional nations can hope to express themselves.

A.M.: Let us return to Switzerland and show why the debate is so hard for us. It is precisely this leap of identification that is more difficult. We are not convinced that we will find everything that we had invested when we arrive.

C.I.: I don't know whether Switzerland is suffering from a sense of insecurity provoked by the question, 'What will become of us if we join Europe, do we have to join, should we perhaps not join?', or if like me, and I am inclined to believe this, the questions the Swiss are asking themselves are side effects, interwoven with other questions.

D.V.: The European issue has certainly brought to the surface all these questions that were more or less latent before.

C.I.: It is curious that every country has its own perception of Europe's role shaped by its own national context. Probably in Switzerland the Swiss have been obliged to address certain questions in the way that we have just outlined. Incidentally these questions underlie the more or less acute political malaise that is affecting every nation in Europe. At the moment no one is living comfortably within a system of guaranteed stability. They all feel a greater or lesser degree of destabilisation in their democratic way of life: in the relationship of citizen to state, in the form of political representation, in questions about their fate within a Europe that is on the move. These questions exist everywhere, but they are dodged, avoided. Switzerland is asking them. And that is in itself remarkable.